TAKING
A YEAR OFF

AN

TROTMAN

This fifth edition published in 2002 by
Trotman and Company Ltd
2 The Green, Richmond, Surrey TW9 1PL
Fourth edition published in 2000
Third edition published in 1997
Second edition published in 1993
First edition published in 1989

© Trotman and Company Limited 2002

British Library Cataloguing in Publication Data
A catalogue record for this book is available from the British Library

ISBN 0 85660 850 5

Typeset by Type Study, Scarborough
Printed and bound in Great Britain by Bell & Bain Ltd

Contents

About the Author

Margaret Flynn is currently a careers adviser at the University of Birmingham and at University College Worcester. She has been involved with personal development planning initiatives at Birmingham over the last ten years, resulting in an interest in how students develop their skills and how time out or a gap year can contribute. She has researched into time out after graduation as part of a master's degree, resulting in a 25,000 word dissertation, has written *Making the Most of Your Gap Year* and written for the *Daily Telegraph*'s 'A Levels and Beyond' supplement.

In editing and rewriting this book, she wishes to acknowledge the extensive work done in earlier editions by Val Butcher and Claire Rees.

Foreword

Taking a year out after school or university has the potential to be one of the most rewarding and exciting times of your life. There are many questions you may, and should, ask yourself when deciding whether to take a gap year. It is not something to rush into but should be thoroughly researched, thought about carefully and planned well to make sure that your adventure is right for you and you gain the most you can from it.

Why take a year out? There are many benefits to taking a gap year. The time off will give you the opportunity to see other parts of the world, you will gain independence and maturity; you can possibly earn money, improve your CV and also have lots of fun! Do remember though that a year is a long time to be away from home, so make sure that you are fully prepared for the experience. Forward planning is the key to making the most of your time away.

What can I do on my gap year? There is a range of options open to you, from teaching in Ghana to working in a ski resort in Canada. You might want to do some voluntary work in an underdeveloped country, be a counsellor on a summer camp, take paid work in a city or learn new skills on courses or work experience closer to home. The wide choices enable you to plan your year off to best suit you.

When can I start my adventure? There is no set time when you have to take your gap year, though some programmes do require you to be a student. You may want to take time off from study before going to university, or once you have completed your degree before beginning work. But it is best to enjoy the adventure while you are still young and don't have too many commitments to stop you.

You don't necessarily have to go away for a whole year either; you could work near home for a few months to earn money to travel, do a course before going abroad or make the most of the whole year off by working on a summer camp before travelling and fitting in as much as possible.

How do I arrange everything? If you have decided that you do want to take a year out you may be daunted by how much you need to sort out before you go. But you don't have to do it all alone. There are many organisations out there to help you decide which adventure is right for you, plan your travels and also offer help and advice while you are abroad. You should do as much research as possible before you go so that you know you have made the right decision and are really well prepared for your time away. A well-planned gap year will probably be one of the most memorable things you ever do.

www.bunac.org

INTRODUCTION

1

A year out at any time can offer you an exciting, challenging and rewarding opportunity, be it in the UK or overseas. It can and probably will enrich your life forever.

Taking a year out has grown in popularity steadily over the past ten years and numbers continue to rise. Universities and employers have noticed the benefits that can be reaped by those who have taken a well-structured year out and many look for it on a CV.

How you choose to spend your year out is up to you. But a well-structured year out does not just happen. For maximum benefit you should set yourself some personal goals for your year and start planning as early as possible.

The number of opportunities available is immense and growing year by year. A few years ago a group of leading year out organisations came together to form the Year Out Group. The Group provides valuable, accurate and impartial information on year out opportunities that will help you make your choice. In addition, its members have all agreed to abide by a Code of Practice which will help to ensure that your year out is a rewarding, safe and enjoyable experience.

Richard Oliver, Chief Executive, Year Out Group
(Website: www.yearoutgroup.org. Tel: 01380 812368)

How popular are gap years?

A record number of university applicants asked to delay their entry to university to take a gap year in 2002 (nearly 26,000, about 7 per cent of all who apply). The number who actually take a gap year is much higher, when you add those who apply to university in their gap year and those who take a gap year after graduation. As an example, the University of Birmingham estimates that about 15 per cent of entrants have taken a gap year and about 7 per cent take a gap year after graduation.

How can this book help?

This book aims to help you find out why gap years are becoming more popular and to make decisions that apply to you.

It will help you:

- **decide if a gap year is for you**
- **consider the main options, highlighting the good and the bad**
- **locate further information sources so you can turn your ideas into reality**
- **decide when to do it**
- **plan for your return.**

As well as deciding what to do with the year, you will need to think about:

- **what you will gain from it**
- **what admissions tutors for degree or other courses think**
- **what employers think**
- **what it will cost**
- **how to get your parents and teachers to give you support.**

This book will provide you with an independent view – based on research and contact with those who are planning and have completed gap years, employers, university and college admissions tutors, teachers and parents. Any organisations featured have had no influence on the content of the book.

All the unattributed quotes from students are from research with University of Birmingham students conducted in the last few years.

As a starting point, look at how one graduate decided on her gap year.

Aruna's profile

Aruna Sethi graduated from the University of Birmingham with a 2.1 degree in Psychology. She took a gap year before university.

'I chose to take a gap year before university because I had an idea of the sort of career I wanted . . . something to do with clinical/educational psychology. I knew that I would have a long path of studying so I decided to take a gap year in order to gain some relevant work experience and have a few adventures along the way!

'I decided not to participate in an organised gap year scheme but to go it alone. I chose the places I wanted to visit, the time I wanted to spend there and the kind of work placements I wanted to be involved in. Looking back I feel proud to have organised each of the placements myself. I think by "going it alone" I have developed my "self-reliance" skills. My self-confidence has also grown. Now I can look back and think, if I did all that on my own I can do anything!

'A good tip for those planning a gap year is to focus your thoughts. Write a simple list of what you would like to do and achieve. I did this and it helped me prioritise my aims and objectives. I also realised that I had to drop some of my ideas as realistically I wouldn't have enough time.

'In the end I managed to gain work experience in England, France, Romania and India. I slotted in a few days' travel in Italy as well. I concentrated on working with adults and children with learning and physical difficulties. Also while in France I spent a month on an intensive language course and a month working in a model agency. My experiences working in a Romanian orphanage were drawn upon in my third year of university when I formatted my dissertation proposal and then went back to the orphanage to carry it out.

'I hope that the relevant experience I gained will help me achieve my aim of becoming an educational psychologist. It was a bonus that I had a great time travelling the world as well!

'I think that I built up my confidence and skills gradually –

my first placement was away from home but still in the UK. I was homesick but it was excellent practice for realising what the pros and cons of living away from home would be. My second placement was in Romania, my third in France and finally I completed three months' work and travel in India. I don't think that I would have coped very well in Romania if I had not had some "practice" at living away from home, especially as the placement in Romania was very demanding.

'I was really keen to pack a lot into my gap year and so I returned to England only five days before university started. In retrospect I don't think this was nearly enough time to settle back into the UK way of life. It would have been better to have left a couple of weeks to reflect on all my experiences and to mentally prepare to move on to the next phase . . . 9am lectures, reading lists and of course cheap drinks at the student union! I rushed this readjustment and so spent several weeks wishing I was back in Romania, France or India. I also think that gap year students need to be slightly cautious of being cynical "hardened travellers" on their return to the UK. Sometimes I think I was more impatient with the usual student moans, eg not being able to go out every night, which seemed trivial to me after working alongside people in extreme poverty who could never afford a night out.

'Gap years are not very common among Asian families. This may be because of the emphasis on education and qualifications combined with strong parental influence. Some parents may not see what you might gain from a gap year. My mum was happy with the idea of a gap year but my dad was more dubious and tried to persuade me to wait until after university.

'I have now graduated from university with a degree but £11,000 of debt! For many people, waiting until after graduation can be impractical, as the debt and pressure to get a foot on the career ladder can dominate. In my case the decision to take a gap year before university was definitely the right one – I had the best year of my life.'

WHY AND WHEN

2

Why take time out?

Taking time out from education or getting off the treadmill appeals to a lot of people. There is much to be gained from visiting new places, getting some useful work experience and trying out something different:

'I feel as though I have done something worthwhile with myself. It would have been easy (but boring) to take six months out and sit around the house doing nothing, but instead I took the initiative and spent six months travelling halfway round the world on my own. That gives me a sense of pride.'

'Like no other time in my life I was totally in control of what I did and what happened to me.'

But be aware of the temptation to drift through 6, 12 or even 24 months. One thing you can be absolutely certain about is that when you return to study, or take up more permanent employment, someone, somewhere, is going to want to know what you did and what you got out of it.

So, how are you going to decide if a year out is right for you?

 Next step

First, produce your own **list of reasons** for considering a gap year.

Then produce a second list of reasons **not** to take a gap year.

Compare the two lists. Which do you feel is more important to you?

Use the ideas listed below to help. They are quotes from young people who have taken a year out.

Why take a year off?	Why not?
it's a break from the education system and you can get rid of exam pressures for a while	your friends get a year ahead of you at university
you get time to rethink your options and time to decide on your course and whether you really want to do it	it was hard to get back into academic study and difficult to settle back into a routine after travelling for a year
you can improve your CV by showing that you have made good use of the time	when I returned to the UK I found I had missed the closing date for application to some companies
you get to see the culture and lifestyles of another country from the inside and maybe learn a language	some college departments don't like you deferring entry
some course tutors like you to have taken time out first	I hoped that a year out would help me decide my

Why take a year off?	Why not?
	career plans, but I still didn't know what I wanted to do when I got back
you broaden your horizons and gain more confidence	it was hard to give up my salary and just do some part-time work alongside my course
you meet lots of different kinds of people	it was difficult to decide whether to give up the job I'd got, as I could have got on in it
you learn to fend for yourself	it was easy to lose touch with friends who'd gone to college earlier
you can gain some relevant work experience	my family weren't keen on the idea
you can earn some money to help pay tuition fees	employers didn't seem impressed with my year out when I went for interviews
doing community work makes you feel you have given something back	
you can travel – you can't do it so easily when you're working or on a course	

In more detail . . .

A group of Year 13 students discuss their plans with a careers tutor. They are considering whether to take a year off after A levels, and before going on to a course of higher education.

'I've always wanted to travel and it seemed a good time to go. I also wanted to make sure that my decision to go on to higher education was the right one and that I'd chosen the right subject. I am planning to study Chinese at university so I want to get some experience of both the language and the country.' (Anita)

'My brother is already at university and my parents can't afford to support both of us in higher education. I need to work to save money towards tuition fees.' (Declan)

'I've had an offer from people I know to work as an au pair in London, and as I want to do teacher training eventually I think it would be a good experience to be with kids for a while, to see how I get on with them!' (Sunita)

'I'm buying time, I want to take a break from education, to get out of the system for a while. After all, I've been in it since I was five! I also need to take a year out before deciding what to do in the future. I've looked through all the prospectuses and just don't seem to be able to find a course that really appeals.' (Leanne)

'I want to do some voluntary work before doing a degree; I think it will help my career later. I'm aiming to be a social worker. Doing some voluntary work will give me good experience and an idea of the challenges I might find in a permanent job after my degree.' (Dev)

'I think graduate recruiters might be impressed that I didn't just stick to the treadmill but made a conscious decision to make use of a year out.' (Delia)

When to do it?

For many people the chance to take time out comes between A levels/Higher grades and university. Some people delay the break until they've finished a diploma or degree course and take a year or more out before going into a job. School/college leavers and graduates seeking employment sometimes find that it takes longer than expected, and want to use the time creatively.

You can also have time out that is built into a sandwich course (which includes a period of work experience related to what you are studying) or your university might arrange shorter periods of work experience for personal development. If your course is flexible enough you might want to organise your own year out. You could delay a gap year until later when your employer may allow a career break or the chance to travel abroad.

This section looks at the three main alternatives of when to take time out:

1. before university
2. after university
3. during your degree.

1. Time out before university

Look at the views expressed below and decide which comments apply to you.

Why take time out now?	Why not take time out now?
after three years of major exams every summer, you need a break	want to get study out of the way in one go
time to decide on a course of higher education – or even if higher education is what you want at all	planning time out during your degree
want to get some work experience relevant to your future course	university department may prefer you to start immediately
spend a year abroad to develop language fluency	don't feel you would get the most out of a gap year now
spend some time away from home before going to university	absolutely cannot afford it
take up a job and save some money to help pay the costs of going to university	

Year 13 students add . . .

'I researched the cost of fees, living expenses etc and I realised that I would have to defer for a year. I felt rather forced into it.' (Declan)

'There should be quite a few benefits. The most obvious one is that I'll get a great insight into life in China before I start my degree (in Chinese). It will really help me to make sure that I've made the right decision course-wise. A year out will make me much more aware of the rest of the world and I'll meet so many new people.' (Anita)

'I think that it will make me more independent and give me a chance to mature. I also feel that a break from study will do me good.' (Declan)

'I'm not sure whether all admissions tutors approve of you taking a year out. Mostly they seem to think it's OK if you do something they think is relevant. But if I do a lot of travelling – or my plans fall through – they might think I've been messing about.' (Dev)

'I'll be living away from home for the first time, which I think will be good for me but will take some getting used to. I will certainly need to learn how to budget more carefully, which will be good practice for life as a student!' (Sunita)

'I think that it will be quite lonely next year. Many of my friends will be at university or working abroad. I'm also a bit worried about finding a job but I'm sure that it will work out in the end.' (Declan)

Martin Shevill, Head of Ossett School and Sixth Form College in Wakefield, who has worked in a university as a tutor on postgraduate teacher training courses, as well as in a variety of schools, offers his personal observations:

'Having worked with both sixth formers and students on teacher training courses who have already completed a degree, I feel that young people tend to do more ambitious things if they take a gap year after their degree. They also seem to be more "worldly-wise" and express themselves more confidently than those who did a gap year after A levels or did not do a gap year at all.

'For some young people the decision to take a gap year before university is the right one. For others, waiting a few years can mean they have the confidence to do more varied, interesting things. Either way, getting the best out of the experiences a gap year has to offer is what is important.'

University students, when asked about the best time to take a gap year, comment:

'Between school and degree, most definitely, because that is the period of your life during which you mature, and you are a much better person for doing it then.' (Ben)

'Yes, I would agree. Looking around, the mature students have a much stronger and more definite approach to their work, and produce better work for it. You have to be strong to come back to study if you've been out too long, but I think you bring so much more with you.' *(Sulima)*

'Also, if you take the break after your degree you have to be sure that you can make a very good job of selling that decision – saying what you've gained, skills and so on. Otherwise you are worse off in the job market. If you take a year off after A levels you have less to lose. On the other hand, some people do change while they are at university and so you may have different ideas about what you want to do when you get to your final year.' (Ben)

'I feel that I'd have wasted a year out after A levels. I'm now more

focused so plan to use my time productively, but maybe it's a question of when you need to take the time out.' (Liz)

'You have to do what is right for you, rather than go along with other people's ideas for your future. In the end it's your decision, it's your life.' (Sulima)

2. Time out after university

Look at the views expressed below and decide which comments apply to you.

Why take time out now?	Why not take time out now?
you've earned it after all those years of study	your future CV could have gaps on it unless you plan your gap year effectively
you need to gain some relevant experience to pursue a particular course or career	employers may not be impressed with your choice of activity during your time out
final exams are tough and applying for jobs plus studying hard can mean too much pressure	if you go abroad you may not be available to attend interviews for jobs or courses
if you don't do it now you never will	you may miss employers' recruiting dates and have to wait until the next round of recruitment the following year
you want to earn some money to pay for postgraduate study	you need to pay off your student debts
you can acquire and develop additional skills to enhance your CV	

Students at university considering a year out:

'I'm going for it! This time it will be much easier to take the decision without feeling that I'm letting someone down. My parents aren't that keen but I feel relaxed about making the most of the opportunities that are out there. I want to take a full-time course in human resource management after my degree but I want to get some more work experience first and save up for the course fees. I don't know if you would say that I am taking time out or starting my career.' (Sulima)

'Money! It has to be the biggest problem. I have to find a way of supporting myself and paying off my overdraft. The worst scenario would be to have to live at home, broke, with my parents getting neurotic.' (Ben)

'I think people are more willing to accept that you are going to take a year out after a degree – because you have got a qualification behind you. A year out for me will be a break from studying, to help me work out where I'm going. I'm not going to sit around and wait for inspiration, though, as I've decided to try and find a temporary job abroad. I don't think that just travelling is the best thing for me. I want to spend some time mixing with local people and learning more about how a country works. I need to brush up my language skills and do some research to help me sort out my longer-term plans.' (Liz)

'I think some employers might think that you'd messed around for a year and not done anything productive. I will have to convince future employers that my time out has helped me make sure that the job I take is a firm choice, that I'll have some commitment to it.' (Liz)

'I'm still thinking about it. I feel that I'm starting my career as I want to try and combine a part-time job with doing some (probably) low or unpaid theatre work. My aim is to get into theatre directing – somehow! But I'm also contemplating doing an MA and have some ideas of where to go after that. I need to make sure that I can afford to do further study. And I could investigate the possibility of doing it part-time. Maybe I'll devote myself to the theatre for a year or two and if at the end of that time I haven't achieved what I want, I'll reconsider.' (Ben)

'I've thought hard about what I might do next year, so I hope that I can convey this to employers when the time comes. I also need to make sure that I can get information on graduate vacancies when I come back. I can find out about some companies via the Internet but I can't guarantee that there will be an Internet café around every corner. I know that I can use the university careers service close to my home to research employers. I'm planning to line up an office skills course as an insurance policy as well.' (Liz)

3. Time out during your degree

Look at the views expressed below and decide which comments apply to you.

Why take time out this way?	Why decide against taking time out this way?
universities often find placements for you	it can make the course longer
you can (sometimes) earn some money during a course	it may be harder to get back into study after a year out
you can get experience relevant to your course and choice of job	you might get a bad placement that puts you off your original choice of career (maybe not a bad thing if you find that out now)
you will improve your personal skills (such as teamworking, time management, communication skills, negotiation) in a different setting	placements (especially short ones) may not necessarily be paid
the placement may lead to sponsorship for the rest of the course	you may have to find your own placements
you get an automatic break from study	you may have to find your own accommodation at home or abroad
employers are likely to rate this experience highly – providing you can talk effectively about what you gained	

Traditionally, 'sandwich' courses provided the opportunities, mainly in language, engineering, science, teaching and business studies. There are now, however, a growing range of 'off-campus placements' and projects – time in the parliament of another country for politics students, for example.

Surveys of employers and graduate recruiters all point up the value of gaining work experience as part of a course.[1] In some cases this can be done through a sandwich course but taking time out in the middle of any course of higher education is becoming easier. You will still need to talk to academic staff to make sure that time out won't be a problem and check out regulations.

Many courses include a period of time away from college, where you can gain industrial experience or experience abroad. Some have exchange schemes operating with other countries, where the programme of study continues, but in a college abroad. This can be a valuable experience for any student, not just those studying languages. Many of these academic exchange schemes are organised in Europe as part of the Erasmus/ Socrates scheme. You can acquire language skills, learn something of the culture of the host country and broaden your perspective.

Philippa's profile

Philippa spent three months working on a research project at the University of Rostock.

'The fact that I could spend some time abroad as part of my biological sciences degree was one of the things that attracted me to the course at the University of Reading. I wanted to work on my final-year project whilst I was abroad and therefore chose to

---

[1] *The 2001 UK Gap Year Report*. Gapyear.com. August 2001.
Time Out: A study of the influences of postgraduation time out on career decision-making, entry into the employment market and career development. Margaret Flynn (Careers Adviser, University of Birmingham). Dissertation for MA in Careers Guidance in Higher Education, University of Reading. March 2002.
Time Well Spent. Community Service Volunteers and Association of Graduate Recruiters. August 2000.
Graduates' Work: Organisational change and students' attributes. Lee Harvey, Sue Moon and Vicki Geall, Centre for Research into Quality, University of Central England in Birmingham. 1997.

spend a term as part of a research team in the Department of Marine Zoology at the University of Rostock in Germany.

'The department organised some language lessons and tapes for the two of us who were going to Rostock but I was glad that I had done GCSE German. This was particularly useful when we arrived in Germany as, due to a mix-up with communications, the administration department was not expecting us. We eventually completed all the relevant paperwork!

'The university has a very well-established Erasmus scheme and there was an excellent support programme for visiting students. I completed a two-week language course and there was also a week of trips and social activities so that we all got to know each other and also something about the country as well. The hall of residence was comfortable and the canteen supplied cheap and good food. The grant we received was adequate and we could afford to explore some more of Germany (plus a weekend in Denmark) in our free time. In fact, when we registered we received a free travel pass, which certainly helped.

'**What did I get out of the experience?** My CV will certainly be more interesting now! I improved my language skills (including my French due to the range of visiting students) and gained a very real insight into a different culture. Rostock is in the former East Germany and it was fascinating to hear about life before reunification. I enjoyed this opportunity to travel and now plan to return this summer to see some more of the country. The experience was very valuable academically, I got the chance to work alongside research staff in a well-known department and gained an insight into the skills needed for this type of work. I was also able to complete my dissertation before returning to Reading after Christmas, unlike my colleagues who were attending lectures and trying to write up their work.'

Sandwich courses

The most common route for a student wanting to combine study with a year out is to choose a degree programme with a 'sandwich course', where the year out is structured into the course. The major advantages are that your department may help to find the placement and you may be paid!

Traditionally, many Applied Science and Engineering degrees have built industrial placements into the degree programme. Dr Clive Souter, from the Centre for Joint Honours in Science at the University of Leeds, comments on the academic advantages of doing a sandwich year:

'The advantages far outweigh any disadvantages for us. We've noticed that students who have done a placement achieve significantly better marks in their final year. Students returning from placements improve their final-year marks, on average, by 5 per cent more than those who have not done a placement. Also, their experience can be ploughed back into the learning of the whole group – they contribute to discussion at a higher level. Third-year students are asked to manage groups of first years in discussions, and 'year out' students have demonstrably greater skills in leading groups.'

There are increasing numbers of non-technical degree programmes that offer 'sandwich' opportunities. One example is the option, in the Department of Politics and International Studies at the University of Leeds, to take a year's placement in a national parliament. Professor David S. Bell explains how the Department came to develop such a scheme:

'We wanted to give students the chance to see how the political system operates from the inside and gain a range of valuable skills, contacts and understandings.

'We have developed a range of placements – with MPs at Westminster, Canadian MPs, Senators and Members of the House of Representatives in Washington, party press offices, parliamentary consultants, in MPs' constituency offices, with European Parliament Members and (we hope soon) in the Scottish and Welsh Parliaments.

'Students have learnt a lot and found the placements very enjoyable. They have been able to develop contacts in the political world, strengthen their CVs, and see how politics works. The placements involve routine, though vital, office work, so that students learn skills that cannot easily be acquired on the academic degree course; students also undertake research work and follow up issues. The placement allows students to pursue topics that they are interested in as well as those that the office requires. There are also unforgettable experiences – in the last couple of years students have been present at a TV interview, campaigned in a by-election in the Canadian West, watched the lorry loads of evidence for the impeachment of President Clinton arrive and visited Paris on an MP's business trip.'

 Next step

After giving some initial thought to why you want time out and when to do it, you now need more detail on the alternatives. Look at the options in the next chapter to help you decide.

THE OPTIONS: WHAT CAN I DO? WHAT WILL IT COST? IS IT FOR ME?

3

What do people do in their gap year?

Most gap year students do a **mix of activities**. This chapter examines the case for and against each option, enhanced by in-depth profiles from people who have already been there and done it. The main options covered are:

1. travel
2. work in the UK
3. work abroad
4. voluntary work
5. study
6. mixing it.

From research done with University of Birmingham graduates who had recently returned from time out,[1] 86 per cent had travelled, 53 per cent had worked in the UK and 51 per cent had worked abroad. Most had combined several activities.

---

[1] *Time Out: A study of the influences of postgraduation time out on career-decision making, entry into the employment market and career development.* Margaret Flynn (Careers Adviser, University of Birmingham). Dissertation for MA in Careers Guidance in Higher Education, University of Reading. March 2002.

Employers in the study indicated they were more impressed by students who took time to plan and structure their gap year and who combined different activities.

1. Travel

> 'I travelled through many South American countries and through many different climates and environments. Although several bad things happened, such as the theft of my rucksack and passport, I enjoyed myself and met many friendly people. One of the most important things I learnt was independence – self-discipline, organisation and coping with different situations by myself.'

Travelling, even for some of the time, is the most popular option. What do you need to consider before you buy your tickets? One graduate suggested that answering the questions which follow is a good starting point. He added that you may not work out some answers until you are halfway round your travels!

1. Do you want to travel alone or with people?

If you travel alone, you answer to nobody, but it's good to have friendly faces around sometimes. If you travel with others, you've always got company so you never feel alone, but you're rarely free to be selfish.

> 'I travelled on my own and loved it. I never felt alone because, on the east coast of Australia, you meet the same people over and over again as you move from place to place.'

2. How 'hard-core' a traveller are you?

Some students suggest 'easier' travelling involves going to places like Australia and New Zealand or the US, which are completely geared up towards the traveller. More demanding places are poorer, non-westernised countries, such as Thailand or Bali. They are used to travellers, but you still have to rough it most of the time. More difficult travelling involves countries such as Cambodia, Laos or some African countries.

3. What do you want out of travelling?

Loads of nights out meeting lots of people? Enjoying yourself but at the same time going places and seeing things? Camping out in the wilds, seeing strange and wonderful landscapes/ animals/people, with no modern conveniences? Choose countries that offer the types of experiences you enjoy most.

What else do you need to think about?

Why go travelling?	Why not?
you can see a lot of the world in six months or a year	it's going to cost you, even if you can get student discounts
it may be your only chance with so much time for travelling or holidays, and it'll be different from a package holiday	if you don't market your experiences positively on a CV or in an interview, the time could just appear self-indulgent or frivolous
you can afford the time to stop and experience places of interest	you could encounter any number of difficult situations, which would require you to 'think on your feet'
things happen abroad, which you will inevitably put down to experience, that should help you to mature and cope with life better	with bad luck you could have money or documents stolen and problems like that are harder to cope with away from home

Why go travelling?	Why not?
you will have a sense of achievement at managing and organising the trip	it's likely you will get ill at some point, again harder to cope with away from home

Here are some more details from 'experienced' travellers.

Jackie's profile

Jackie waited until she had finished her degree studies before taking a year out to 'travel the world'.

'I did a lot of preparation – reading books from the library and in my university careers service. I went along to a travel agent and found out about the variety of routes that included South East Asia. I did some general research. Most of the information I got was from embassies and talking to people who had done it.

'At the time I was horrified at the idea of going on my own and spent a great deal of effort trying to persuade people to go with me. Now I'd say that was the biggest mistake I made, in the sense that I think I got most out of it being on my own. I think I got far more out of travelling on my own than I would have done in company – you meet a lot more interesting people when you are on your own than you do when you have the security of someone with you.

'One of the biggest problems I encountered was getting ill. It's almost standard that anyone who travels at that sort of level, certainly in Asia or other developing countries, is going to get ill at some time, usually with diarrhoea, so you tend to accept it as part of the package. I was laid up with dysentery for a month in Nepal. I was in bed for ten days and was very weak and could hardly eat or drink. It took me about two and a half weeks to recover.

'The other things that had worried me were personal harassment, having my money stolen, being a woman alone, getting raped or attacked. I wouldn't say you shouldn't think about them as the fact that I considered them made me safer. I did meet a lot of people who had had travellers cheques and cameras stolen – many were sitting in hotels, waiting for American Express to reimburse them. But mostly if you were sensible and kept your ears and eyes open and knew where these sorts of things happened you could generally get by safely.

'One thing I found invaluable was a padlock, because if you are sleeping out on your own you have to padlock your valuables to you, or to a wall, or to the bed, and it's useful to lock people out of your room, so a variety of locks is useful. But if I had to go with one thing it would be a guidebook. I know some people disapprove of the idea of a guidebook because it defines everything you should see, but I think I would have found it more difficult without one.

'I'd say not to be put off, worried or frightened by the idea. It's much easier than you think. There are a million and a half people doing it and you think you are going to be the only one out there – a pioneer in India with your backpack! Then at the first hotel you meet just hundreds of people all doing the same, and they all speak English! What I would say is that it's going to be the most rewarding thing you could do. And if you don't like it you can always catch the next flight home!'

Steve's profile

Steve, a geography graduate, has returned from time out and reflects on his experiences.

'It's one of those things that was amazing at the time, but seems even better when you get home and return to routine life and think back to what it was like. For me it was such a good thing because you have to be totally independent – even if you are travelling with someone else. Like no other time in my life I was totally in control of what I did and what happened to me. At any one time no one in the world really knew where I was and there was no one to tell me what I should or should not do and where I should go – every decision was determined by what I felt like doing at the time. That's not to say you are alone – you meet loads of people from many different countries, cultures and beliefs, but fundamentally everything is down to you.

'Filling time was one of the less glamorous aspects. People

think that travelling is one big holiday – yes, you do see loads of amazing things, and have a brilliant time, but it's also very hard work – I was constantly on the move and rarely stayed in one place for more than a few days. Travelling involves lots of long bus journeys (24 hours was my worst), lots of sitting around, and often just trying to entertain yourself and pass many long hours. Possibly the most essential travel item was my pack of cards, so that I could pass the time whilst meeting other people. Other important items for the buses etc are a personal stereo and books.

'Things like e-mail and TV are always there and are good when you feel down and just want a bit of normality. One thing is for sure – when you get home you soon forget about all the waiting around and the times you were bored – all the memories will be good!

'I don't really think I can say how I dealt with the ups and downs – my feelings were that I just had to deal with them. The ups are easy because there are so many – every time you try something new, meet another traveller or do something you never thought you would have the guts to do. The downs – it is sometimes hard. There were times when I was bored and wanted to be somewhere else, but these times just helped the ups seem even better! When I felt down or things seemed bad I just took a step back and thought where I was and what I was doing. I thought about the things I had done and things I had lined up to do – this usually brought a smile. There's no doubt there are hard times but that's all part and parcel of travelling – it's full of challenges that make it an experience you will never forget. I can guarantee if there is a time when it all goes wrong – you're stuck in the middle of nowhere sleeping in the car, freezing, lost, no food – those are the times that you will recite to people and laugh about the most.'

Spike's profile

Spike advises on basic precautions.

'I've just come back from a six-month trip to the south of France and Spain. I had a great time and I hope your trip is trouble free. There are a few basic precautions that it's sensible to take. For example, don't keep all your money in one wallet; take a few travellers cheques and shop around for good insurance for a long trip. I also carried a credit card, for emergencies only. I know it can be a hassle if you have it stolen but it is another means of paying for food or accommodation if you are really stuck. In an emergency the British Consulate or Embassy will help you get in touch with your family, who should be able to get money out to you through some of the banks. They will also try to help if your passport is stolen. But they won't loan or give you money.'

If you are still interested in travelling as part of your year, try this quiz to help you decide if you can cope with the ups and downs of travelling.

The 'Travelling – Can you Cope?' Quiz

1. You know you will be stopping off in a remote part of Borneo where there are few foreigners. Do you:
   a pack your electronic currency calculator
   b make contact with someone just returned from there via the gapyear.com website and get a list of dos and don'ts
   c spend hours researching everything about the country – culture, geography, history, language etc?

2. You book an overnight sleeper on the train from Prague to Krakow. Then you hear stories about crime on the route, including one about being knocked out by gas put in the air conditioning system. Do you:
   a decide to stay up all night protecting your belongings
   b buy an extra padlock and decide to try and get some rest, but realise you probably won't get much sleep anyway what with the noise of the train and interruptions from passport officials
   c cancel your booking?

3. You've already travelled to several countries, then at the next border the passport officials won't let you enter. They say your name is on a list of suspect people denied entry, even though your date and place of birth are different. Do you:

a   offer them a bribe
b   turn back and find the British Embassy to help
c   go home to sort it out in case the same thing happens again?

4. You've heard Nepal is a friendly and beautiful place to visit. Do you:

a   include it in your flight itinerary
b   remember hearing about problems there recently, so you check with the 'Know Before You Go' website
c   research all the newspaper reports for the last two years, ask a friend who went there ten years ago to tell you about it, then decide to avoid it, even if it was going to be your main route into Tibet?

5. You want a year travelling abroad but haven't enough money. Do you:

a   pay a deposit for the ticket and hope your parents will come up trumps nearer the time
b   find out how much you'll need for the whole trip and start saving
c   get a job, and put by £1000 before you look into it again?

6. You are female and travel to Morocco for the first time. You get a lot of unwanted male attention. Do you:

a   ask around the hotel/hostel for anyone with the same problem and go out and about with them
b   assume it is because of the skimpy top and shorts you are wearing, so change to a long sleeved top and long skirt when you next go out
c   don't go out unless forced and move on to another country quickly?

7. You're worried about being mugged. Do you:

a   keep all your money, travellers cheques, passport etc in the same pocket in your rucksack
b   keep most of it in the same place where you constantly watch it, but separate some things, like travellers cheques and tickets
c   keep all of it in different places, and a credit card in your sock?

8. You decide to allay your parents' worries by agreeing to keep in regular touch with them. Do you:

   a   tell them you'll be in touch when you need more funds
   b   agree to ring every 2–3 weeks, but do not give a definite time, just in case you can't get to a phone and they worry too much as a result
   c   tell them you will ring at 6pm every Friday?

How did you get on?

Mainly a: you tend to be a bit rash and go over the top on some things and give no thought to others. This could get you into tricky situations when travelling!

Mainly b: you weigh up the pros and cons before making decisions to take calculated risks and, providing you don't take too long deciding, you could enjoy travelling.

Mainly c: you tend to be over cautious, but could enjoy it if you lighten up a little.

Next step

If travelling appeals to you, think about how much money you will need.

Money issues

'Anyone thinking about travelling? . . . Then go for it – it will be the best thing you ever do in terms of finding out about yourself and what you want in life. Another thing – think seriously about how you are going to fund it. I'm so glad I came back with no debt, whereas I know loads of people who've returned with £2000–3000 debt.'

One reason for people not doing a gap year is cost. But do you know how much it will cost? In April 2002 Trailfinders

advertised round the world tickets from £721. The Gapyear
Company website suggests upward of £700 is the norm.

A student who travelled to Thailand, Malaysia, Australia,
New Zealand, Cook Islands and the US in 2000 calculated:

> 'The whole trip, if I count all the expense incurred after the
> flight and deduct what I earned in Sydney, cost about £2000.
> Not bad for ten months.'

A more extravagant student went in 2000 to South East Asia and
Australia.

> 'I went for ten weeks with two friends and spent about
> £3000. We did not work at all and did absolutely
> everything.'

These differences show that **further research** is a must:

- **Contact a student travel specialist such as Trailfinders or STA.**
- **Look on the Internet and in weekend newspapers for details of flights.**
- **Buy the relevant travel guides, eg Lonely Planet or Rough Guides. Check their websites.**
- **Use the budgeting section of the gapyear.com website.**

 Next step

Still not sure about travelling? Try it out for a couple of
weeks next holiday and see how it goes. Borrow a backpack
and go travelling in Europe or in the UK.

---

2. Work in the UK

Just a means to an end?

Some students need to spend time working, to fund other things they want to do in their gap year or to help pay university expenses. Many students find some of the jobs they get dull and routine. Does it matter? How will that look on your CV?

'I got a job in a bank from an employment agency for seven months, filling that in with bar work and any other casual work to make the money I needed (ie I put leaflets around the area I lived and obtained several handyman jobs etc). I basically lived like a hermit for that time and saved every possible penny – it was hard but I could do it because I knew it was a means to an end and that I was doing it for a very good reason.'

'I spent a couple of months at home (not working) to "recover" from my final exams and spent the remainder of the year doing various temping jobs . . . I worked for seven months in a call centre as a salesperson and in customer services and learnt a lot of new interpersonal skills. Following this I ran all the admin for a small office for a month and then worked for three months in an invoicing department and I made lots of new friends. My main gains throughout the year were learning to work with a wide range of different people and to be flexible.'

Be prepared to accept routine work. It's only for a limited time, you will gain an insight into working practices in different industries and it's a great opportunity to improve your personal skills, such as teamworking, telephone skills or dealing with the public. It may turn out to be better experience than you think.

Julie's profile

'The year that I was due to start university, I found out in August that I needed urgent surgery to both knees. I was panic-stricken and didn't know what to do so called a national careers helpline. I took their advice and deferred my place for a year, which I hadn't realised you could do at the last minute.

'Although the decision was not my choice, I decided to use this time to my advantage and secured employment for six months (in between operations) as an administrative assistant within the Civil Service. I worked in a large team, in a client-focused environment, which developed my communication, teamworking and organisational skills.

'This employment gave me the opportunity to save up some money for the all-important fresher social life and to improve my confidence and interpersonal skills.

'When I started my business studies course I found that I was able to grasp coursework quicker and with a fuller understanding as I had some real work experience to apply to the theory. The contacts that I made and the experience I had gained within the organisation helped secure employment with them for the following four vacations, which came in very handy for appeasing the bank manager!

'Although I was very upset when I realised that I would have to wait a year to go to university, I quickly realised how much I had benefited from the experience. Now, several years on, I am an information manager within an education establishment, and I am still using and developing the skills that I obtained during my gap year.'

Useful career-related experience?

Some students choose to spend a year gaining valuable work experience with one employer, relevant to the subject they intend to study at university or to their future career plans.

'On leaving university I had no money, no plans and no ties. I didn't want to go off anywhere with no money and started looking for a temporary job. I ended up working in my local authority – a job which proved to be interesting and offered me invaluable experience. I learnt so much whilst working there that I now have plenty of skills and experience for my CV. I would definitely recommend searching for such a job – factory work may bring in fast money but you can't refer to it continually in interviews.'

If you decide on a gap year before university you could use the opportunity to apply for a sponsorship scheme, where the employer will also offer you some financial support on your degree course and vacation work. Your careers teacher or local careers/Connexions service should have details of organisations that offer sponsorship.

You could apply to 'The Year in Industry' – the only organisation that provides structured, challenging and **paid** employment in the UK for students, mainly in engineering, business, science or IT. The Smallpeice Trust offers work experience in the UK and a placement in Europe.

'Right from the start I had some major tasks to complete – in my first few weeks I completed a solo visit to the production plant of Jaguar. I learnt lots about assembly processes – and about staff reactions.' (Year in Industry student)

'The Year in Industry' scheme helps students to find gap year placements with a range of organisations. Salaries range from about £9000–11000 pa or more and some students also secure longer-term sponsorship. Additional management training is included. A number of students have also travelled abroad as part of the programme. It is supported by all university admissions tutors and in 2001 26 per cent of ex-Year in Industry students gained a first class Honours degree, compared with approximately 10 per cent of other students.

Alex's profile

Alex Wilson, who is now studying for a degree in French, decided to apply for the programme so that she could gain some experience of the real world and to put a distance between studying before going to university. Alex felt that she would not only earn some money on the scheme but also gain some valuable experience in managing her finances and budgeting. Finally, the experience gained through her placement would, she believed, enhance her CV.

Alex took a one-year placement at Zeta Communications – designers and manufacturers of voice and data communication products. Initially her work was solely concerned with marketing, but then she took on market research, some finance and also sales. Looking back on her time with Zeta, Alex believes that this experience enabled her to become more mature and also renewed her determination to go on to higher education. She could now see, much more clearly, the benefits of higher education and how these could be related to a work environment. Employers have looked very favourably on Alex's experience. She has already obtained two vacation jobs whilst at university on the strength of her time with Zeta.

Laurence's profile

Laurence used this scheme to help him get a job with National Grid, which owns and operates the high-voltage electricity transmission system in England and Wales, before going to Queens' College, Cambridge, to read for an MEng.

'It gives a good break from exams and academic work; it's good to earn a reasonable amount of money before becoming a student; and it's much more interesting and useful than just working in a shop for the year. If you want sponsorship for your degree course you're more likely to be able to get it after a year working for a company.

'I got much better at using computers, managing work myself and meeting deadlines. Communication skills such as getting your message across on the phone clearly and giving effective presentations, also improve. Teamworking is another skill that is useful for just about every other job you do.

'You also pick up other things that don't give CV points, such as more self-confidence, and understanding what office politics is really all about!'

A year becomes 2, 3, 4 . . . ?

For some it could mean taking more than just a year out. The intention may be to delay going on to a higher education course for one year, but some people find that they like the job they have taken up. It may offer the chance of getting higher qualifications, so you could decide to stay in it for a while longer. After all, the money comes in handy. So this is the risk you take if you go into employment – you may end up deciding not to bother with higher education at all, or to return to university after several years. Sarah comments as follows.

Sarah's profile

'I left school at 18 after completing my A levels. I had achieved good grades and, whilst my parents never pressured me, my teachers naturally expected me to continue my education at university. For my part I had no clear idea about what I wanted to do, but knew that I needed a break from studying. I always knew I could return to further education, but only if and when the time was right.

'I signed up with a local recruitment agency, and before long had myself a job as an administrator at a firm of financial advisers. Whilst this was never going to be a long-term career choice I enjoyed my job and was able to employ many of my existing skills and learn new ones.

'I was responsible for my own workload, but also formed part of a larger team, which improved my time management and organisational skills as well as introducing me to the concept of teamwork. I gained experience in dealing with people of all ages and backgrounds, which improved my interpersonal skills, and a proportion of my job involved problem solving for our clients, an aspect that became increasingly satisfying.

'After a few years I began to think again about further education and became very interested in one career in particular – physiotherapy, a degree-based career. Once I was studying from choice I found myself committed to learning and had no difficulties organising my studies and meeting deadlines after my years in administration.

'I have been qualified for two years now, and work at a large teaching hospital. I thoroughly enjoy my job, and know that I have chosen the right career. I don't regret any of my previous choices, and recognise the many transferable skills learned during my working years. It perhaps wasn't the easiest move, from salaried employee to full-time student, but in the long run it was definitely the right one!'

Is work an option for you?

If you are thinking of working in the UK as part of your gap year look at the cases for and against to help you decide.

Why work in the UK?	Why not?
you can earn some money to use for holidays or to finance university studies	you may be earning money, but you'll be expected to pay for your keep, and for lodgings if away from home
you can take a break from education to see how the 'nine-to-fivers' live	you end up a year behind your friends who went off to university before you
you can gain experience that will help your practical understanding of a subject you wish to study later on	you may struggle with the routine of the job, being tied to working hours
taking responsibility in a job helps you to mature	you can get used to earning decent money, which might be hard to give up when you become a student
you can learn a great deal about yourself, how you	you may find it difficult to get the right job, and feel

Why work in the UK?	Why not?
work with others, cope with routine and tackle problems	that you are wasting valuable time doing very routine work
employer contacts you make could be useful when you are ready to take up a permanent career	the job situation may make it difficult for you to find the right kind of job
you may get the chance to take extra qualifications, which may help later when you want a job in university vacations	

If you have decided to try and work at least some of the time, what next?

Where to look for jobs?

- **local papers: most put their job vacancies on www.fish4jobs.co.uk**
- **local careers company or Connexions service (www.connexions.gov.uk)**
- **Jobcentre Plus offices and websites: www.worktrain.gov.uk, www.jobcentreplus.gov.uk**
- **magazines, eg *Community Care* for work in social care**
- **recruitment or employment agencies**
- **personal contacts: don't be shy to ask people you know**
- **write to companies direct, using specialist directories in your local library for addresses**
- **college/school job shop (if you have one)**
- **your university careers centre (for graduates).**

What if you can't find a job straight away?

When you are 18 and have left school or college you can register as unemployed with your local Jobcentre Plus and may be eligible for Job Seekers Allowance. Currently the rate of benefits for most people at 18 is about £42 a week, but this depends on certain conditions, such as the amount of your savings.

You have to remain 'ready, willing and able to work' whilst registered, but you can do voluntary work and may be able to take advantage of special training or get reduced rates or free entry to some courses at your local college of further education. Sports and cultural facilities may be cheaper to use, and there may be support groups locally for unemployed people. You can find out about opportunities for voluntary work through your local volunteer centre.

What if you can't find any work?

After six months you may be eligible to join more formal work experience training opportunities. These could include work-based learning with an employer, training in specific skills such as information technology or workshop sessions on finding a job. Information on the options open to you should be available from your Jobcentre Plus. If you have recently left school or college then your local careers/Connexions service may also be able to help.

Check for up-to-date details on the Department for Work and Pensions website (www.dfwp.gov.uk).

Graduates should contact the careers service at their local university; you may be able to use some of the resources there even if you attended another institution. Check for details on www.prospects.ac.uk.

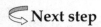 **Next step**

- **Check out the websites and other sources of job vacancies.**
- **Talk to careers staff for ideas.**

---

3. Work abroad

'I obtained a working visa for Canada through BUNAC.
I flew to Vancouver in September and spent a few weeks
travelling . . . got a job in the sales and marketing
department of a ski resort. Did a variety of roles (sales,
marketing, promotions, ski guiding), skied lots, all in an
amazing setting.'

You can do more than bar work or fruit picking. The range of
jobs people do on a gap year is huge. Many are casual or
temporary jobs, picked up at short notice, but if regular
employment is what you are after then a good deal of planning
ahead needs to be done.

The research done with University of Birmingham students
shows a wide range of job opportunities:

- **teaching English in China for six months**
- **football coaching in the US**
- **working on a ranch in the US**
- **kitchen work in Canada (ski season)**
- **teaching English in Japan**
- **delivering leaflets in Australia**
- **waitressing in Australia.**

What can be said in favour of or against working abroad?

Why work abroad?	Why not?
your future career may offer no chance of working abroad, so taking time out might give you your only opportunity to live and work abroad for a time	it will cost you – fares to and from the country, as well as travelling around within it
you can see another country and its culture from close quarters – and that's	you could get homesick and miss your friends and the social life you have at home

40

Why work abroad?	Why not?
different from being on holiday	
it can provide an opportunity to learn or brush up on language skills, unless you are in an English-speaking country	it can be difficult to obtain work permits for some countries outside Europe
you may broaden your horizons and outlook generally	it can be lonely until you meet people and sort out a new social life
you can gain employment experience useful to your career	you could get out of the habit of studying and find it hard to resume if you are going back into education
you could find the time to travel around your host country	it could turn out to be all work and little play

Now read about how three students felt about their experiences working abroad.

Megan's profile

Before she goes:
'I'm finally getting organised with the trip to Australia.
'I'm hoping to work for at least some of the time – have to really, because I can't save that much before we go! I need a Working Holiday Visa, which allows me to travel for 12 months, but to work at the same time – as long as I don't work for the same employer for more than three months. Sounds ideal! I've heard that the chances of finding a job are pretty good if I am flexible. Someone also said that jobs such as fruit picking tend to be available even if others aren't. I'm prepared to go where the jobs are and plan to arrive with good references and CV at the

ready, so there should be plenty of casual work about. But it's still difficult to know what to expect.

'I've been saving like crazy just in case. The fare was going to cost about £700–800 at the time I want to fly, and I need to have some £2000 put by as a guarantee (a condition of the visa).'

And while she is there:

'At the hostel there was a noticeboard for jobs, so I got some work shortly after I arrived. I did a very basic clerical job for a few weeks with a bus company, and later some leafleting for a dry cleaning company – handing out promotional material to commuters every morning as they came out of the station.

'After six weeks I headed north for Brisbane, and ended up working in a resort called Surfer's Paradise, this time as a waitress. When I wasn't working I tried out all kinds of things – from windsurfing to bungee jumps. And went with friends to the mountains – lots of waterfalls, wildlife and a rainforest climate. Four of us got a flat together in the end.

'Getting a job has not been as difficult as I expected – maybe because I told everyone I met from day one that I was looking for work. I soon learned not to expect anything too grand – waitressing and bar work are the norm. At the start I signed on with lots of agencies for typing work, but most of the better jobs go to people with experience. The main thing is that I've managed to pick up enough work to stay solvent.'

Vajeeha's profile

Vajeeha had always been interested in travelling, but spending her holidays in even the most exotic places was no longer enough. Wanting to experience living abroad rather than just visiting, she chose to spend two years in Japan on the JET Programme as an assistant language teacher.

'Although most JETs tend to be recent graduates, I went on the programme three years after completing my studies. I had a lot of travel experience, but was looking for a way to combine work with travel in order to fund the trip and experience a country as more than just a tourist. Having always thought that teaching English would be a good way to do so, I was naturally very interested when I heard about the JET Programme.

'Former JETs recommended the many benefits of the programme: visas, accommodation, work, return travel, hotel conference and more – it all sounded too good to be true.

'The application process was rigorous but definitely worth it. I applied in November and by April I was notified of my acceptance and placement in Amagasaki, in Hyogo-Ken – just an hour from Kyoto. I was thrilled to be accepted and to be placed in an area I had requested – the location was perfect for me.

'As the departure date approached I felt apprehensive about not knowing any Japanese, as well as whether some of the basic amenities taken for granted in my culture would also be found in such a different one. For example, what kind of toilet would I have? Primitive squat-style or a more high-tech, western device? To my relief such worries proved unfounded, as I found people to be very friendly and patient in working with the language barrier, and my housing was great – government sponsored and only £20 a month (and I had a western-style toilet!).

'I taught at two senior high schools. One was full of young boys with punk hairstyles, body piercings and plucked eyebrows! The last thing they wanted to do was learn English, but I nevertheless really enjoyed teaching them as they were more outspoken than the stereotypical shy student I was led to expect. My other school had a strong "international" programme and was more progressive in its teaching style.

'In both schools I enjoyed helping out in some of the many after-school clubs and festivals, including helping students prepare for speech competitions. It was great to be able to get the traditionally shy students to open up to non-Japanese ideas, as well as for me to learn more about Japanese people and culture.

'In addition to earning a great boost to my CV I was also able to make the most of my travel opportunities. As well as seeing a lot of Japan I managed to visit South Korea, Vietnam, Hong Kong, Malaysia, Thailand and the Philippines. That's something I really miss now.

'I have so many wonderful memories of the programme – little things like late-night karaoke and green tea ice cream. I'll also always remember the time a former student called me to say thanks for something I'd taught him (it helped him at university), helping me to realise what a difference my work made – an experience that no two-week holiday can provide.

'Professionally, the JET experience has definitely provided a talking point on my CV, and ultimately helped me to land a job back home with CIEE, who administer the programme. And it's funny how one international experience can lead to another – I'm now moving to CIEE's Boston Office in the US.

'All in all JET is a wonderful programme, and an experience that I would heartily recommend. Just go with an open mind and make the most of it!'

Catherine's profile

'When I came to make my choice of which university to go to and what to study I realised I had followed the natural progression from school into sixth form and then on to university. I wanted to be sure I actually wanted to go to uni myself and not simply follow what everyone else was doing. My eldest brother had taken a gap year and travelled and I think his experience had influenced my decision. I also wanted to take some time out from studying following my exams.

'From September until February I worked in the kitchen of a restaurant full time to earn some money to travel. After that I participated on the BUNAC Work Canada programme and spent five months working in the Canadian Rockies out West.

'At the time I was a keen skier and was interested in becoming a ski instructor. All I wanted to do with my gap year was ski, so I started to research about working in a ski resort. I was reading a book called *How to Get a Job in a Ski Resort* that mentioned BUNAC so I contacted them and learned a little more about the programmes they ran and it sounded like the ideal opportunity. I would be able to work as well as travel. I didn't have to raise the large amount of money required by some of the voluntary programmes I had looked at doing, I could work in an English-speaking country and it was relatively affordable on my budget. It all happened very quickly and before I knew it I was on the plane to Vancouver.

'What did I gain from the experience? Independence, patience, resilience – to name a few things. I grew up a lot in a short space of time, as it was the first time I had lived away from home and away from my family. I had a great sense of achievement when I returned to know that I had lived on my own in a foreign country for five months, something I felt quite proud about. I also gained valuable work experience, something that I hope will enhance my employability when I apply for jobs in the future.

'There is no doubt I had ups and downs during my time away. The most exciting part was meeting new people who were all doing a similar thing, just wanting to have a good time and do things. I got to see so many places, meet so many people of different nationalities and live in some of the world's most beautiful places. I got to be more than a tourist, see places in a different light, and we even got called locals by the end of our stay due to the fact we were working over there!

'I'm sure there were many low points, many of which you tend to forget or pass over and just remember all the good things. I had to finish the first job I had taken as the ski season had come to an end and then look for another job during the peak summer period. This took me a week, during which time I had to stay in a youth hostel. It was particularly difficult being away from home and family at this time. I would talk to my parents regularly and, using all the info and advice I was given, landed up being offered three jobs in one day!

'When you are in these situations when you travel you realise that no one else will do things for you – it is up to you to get things done, so you do them without thinking twice about it.'

Working means taking on all the responsibilities for living, tax etc **on your own**. Try this quiz to see if it's a realistic option for you.

The 'Work Abroad – Can you Cope?' Quiz

1. You want to go to Australia on a student 'work and travel visa'. Do you:

   a assume there will be jobs put aside especially for people like you

   b take a recent CV, a decent pair of trousers and register with agencies as soon as you arrive

   c take a smart suit and shoes, rent a room in a house as soon as you arrive, register with agencies and thoroughly research all the companies that interest you?

2. You want to teach English as a Foreign Language abroad, so do you:

   a choose a country where you think there will be demand and contact all the language schools when you get there

   b do a 'taster' course that costs a couple of hundred pounds to see if you like it and apply to organisations which let you teach for a few months without having a more in-depth qualification

   c discover many jobs want a TEFL qualification, which can cost £1000 and takes a month, so decide it's too expensive and give up the idea?

3. You won't be 18 until the end of July and you want to work abroad, preferably on an organised scheme. Do you:

   a assume you can apply at 17

   b check out the age limits on schemes that interest you, before you start filling out forms to apply

   c don't apply for anything until after your birthday?

4. You want to go to the US but have very little money. Do you:

   a give up the idea and stick closer to home

   b look for schemes that pay for your flight and then recoup it from your salary, still leaving you a reasonable amount to live on

   c go through *Petersen's Internships* with a fine toothcomb, assessing how much you will earn, and then try and get a loan to cover the air fare?

5. You realise most countries have entry regulations (visas, work permits etc). Do you:

   a assume students are not affected by this

   b look up all the relevant details on embassies' websites, and make sure you have the right documents in advance

   c get all the forms you can think of and lose heart at the sixth one?

6. You've never done any babysitting or shown any interest in children, but are thinking of applying to be an au pair abroad. Do you:

a   apply – children can't be that bad, especially in small numbers

b   decide to get some experience of small children locally (eg at Brownies or a local playgroup) to see how you get on with them

c   decide against it – after all you've heard about cases where au pairs are treated unfairly?

7. You like the idea of a summer working on a ranch in the US. You realise it is difficult to get a visa for the US, so do you:

a   decide to wait until you get there and then look for a job

b   decide to contact one of the official legal sponsors, eg Council Exchanges or BUNAC, realise they have a database of employers you can use to contact ranches and so decide their fee is worth it and apply

c   spend hours searching the Web for details of ranches in the US and contact them for possible jobs. You also decide to get a US visa yourself, even though the bureaucracy is daunting?

How did you get on?

Mainly a: you tend to give little thought to preparation and trust to luck. This may pay off, but it may not, and it could lead you into some sticky situations.

Mainly b: you make good preparations but are still willing to have a go when the situation demands it. This attitude would be an asset when working abroad.

Mainly c: you prefer to be cautious and go the long way round when looking for solutions. Would you get too bogged down and not enjoy the experience?

If working is something you want to include on your itinerary, then what is the next step?

How to find a job

You could:

- **Get help through one of the gap year organisations such as BUNAC, Council Exchanges or i to i. You pay a fee for their services, which include providing you with either jobs or access to a list of employers for you to contact**

directly. Get a deferred entry place at university if you want to go abroad on an organised scheme. Some schemes, eg BUNAC, make this a requirement. Most organisations have websites: start with www.yearoutgroup.org.

- **Sort out any visa requirements before you go, then look for a job on arrival, eg through a recruitment agency.**
- **Arrange a job before you go, using websites or books such as *Summer Jobs Abroad*.**

What can you expect to get paid?

How much do you need to survive in the countries where you plan to work?

Travel guides (eg Lonely Planet or Rough Guides) usually give an idea of living costs. Some gap year organisations can also provide information. For example, BUNAC state that people on their Work Australia scheme earn about $360 (Australian) a week and pay about $160 for food and accommodation.

Make some contingency plans – what if you get the sack? Have you enough to live on? Can you change your travel arrangements to move on more quickly, perhaps to a cheaper place/country?

⬅ **Next step**

- **Investigate organisations that can help.**
- **Look at some of the references listed in Chapter 10 – Factfile.**
- **Think about contingency plans.**

---

4. Voluntary work

What do you know about voluntary work?

Did you know:

- **you often get an allowance and accommodation thrown in?**
- **voluntary work opportunities are available at home and abroad?**
- **you usually need to plan voluntary work in advance, through a charity or voluntary organisation?**
- **there is a wide range of types of work you can do?**

For voluntary work abroad you often have to pay a fee, which can be quite substantial, eg £2700 with SPW (Students Partnership Worldwide). You are expected to fundraise to help with costs and most organisations give help with ideas.

The range of activities available is much wider than most people realise. Some voluntary work is more 'expeditionary' such as Raleigh International, Coral Cay, Frontier or Trekforce, and often based on conservation issues. Others are run by religious organisations and would expect a certain level of faith to join, eg Right Hand Trust. Gap Activity Projects run social work, conservation and teaching projects. Inter-Cultural Youth Exchange run placements involved with drug rehabilitation

programmes, working with street children, human rights projects and HIV programmes.

At home there are national organisations, such as CSV (Community Service Volunteers), which find you placements. Local ones exist, such as the Treloar Trust in Hampshire, where you can gain experience in classrooms, medical centres and sports and therapy departments. International organisations such as Oxfam offer volunteer placements in the UK.

See Chapter 10 – Factfile – for details of these and other voluntary opportunities.

What can I do?

'I decided to go with GAP to teach English as a Foreign Language in northern India for three months. The fact that GAP has a lot of experience in arranging placements and that it is a charity were important to me – you are not paying towards company profits, as GAP is run for and by volunteers. Once there, being flexible was key. I got involved in putting on a play, teaching art in the lower school and Hamlet to sixth formers as well as TEFL! There's nothing like living in a place to genuinely experience the culture of a country.'

'I spent three months in Tanzania . . . I was part of a group helping to build a new school classroom in three rural villages. We also had the opportunity to go into the villagers' homes, play sports with the children and give English lessons. From this experience I have developed the ability to work with others as part of a team in a very different environment.'

Graeme's profile

Graeme Usher worked in Brazil with ICYE (Inter-Cultural Youth Exchange).

'I decided last year that I wanted to do something for the good of our world, while at the same time giving myself the opportunity to broaden my horizons. After deciding that I wanted to work either with children or on an environmental project, and sifting through various sending organisations . . . I finally decided on going with ICYE. The reason I chose ICYE was because I liked its mission statement and the people involved.

'After looking over the various options they offered, I decided that I wanted to work with disadvantaged children in Brazil. The project offered to me was working in a non-profit crèche, in the city of Porto Alegre, in the most southern state of Brazil. My work in the project was not only being involved with the children but attempting to fundraise internationally for them so that they could complete a gymnasium. The previous fundraising activities were seriously hampered due to no one in the crèche being able to speak English. Therefore I took on the task of attempting to raise the £10,000 required for the completion of the gym.

'The most challenging part of the whole experience was overcoming the language barrier (I never spoke a word of Portuguese before I went) and adjusting to living within a family environment again.

'However, out of the whole experience, I can now speak Portuguese (sort of), I have a greater understanding of the plight of truly impoverished people and a wide knowledge of the geography and diverse cultures present in Brazil. I also got a sense of achievement as the letters promising funds arrived . . . it felt as though I had actually done something to improve their standard of living (even though it was just in a small way).'

Tim's profile

The Karen Hilltribes Trust (KHT) accepts motivated and capable young people for six months to assist with teaching English and working on the installation of potable water systems in the remote hills of north-west Thailand. The cost is about £1000.

Tim Hodges, a graduate from St Andrews University, spent six months living and working as a volunteer with the Karen people. He travelled out with five other volunteers, some in their gap year, some after graduation.

'The prospect of standing in front of 40 Thai kids and teaching them English filled me with trepidation. I was excited about the challenge, but with no teacher training experience whatsoever, to say I felt a bit daunted is something of an understatement. I spoke no Thai, and had been told that the level of English of the children was low. What on earth would I do? However, I prepared some sample lesson plans and ideas with other volunteers before we started. It was great to bounce ideas off one another, and also reassuring to know that I was not the only one worried about the teaching. The first few lessons were nerve-racking, but I got through them, thinking on my feet and off the top of my head a lot of the time. Long-forgotten children's songs popped into my memory at just the right time, and handy hints from previous volunteers also came in very useful.

'The Karen Hilltribes Trust is a small charity, based in York, that works with the Karen Hilltribe people who live in the mountainous forest regions of Northern Thailand. The Karen are an indigenous tribe, made up largely of subsistence farmers living in remote villages, often without clean water or electricity. KHT provides opportunities for volunteers to help with teaching and setting up water projects in the area. In June 2001 I went to meet the Trust's director, Mrs Penelope Worsley, and before I knew it I was making arrangements to leave for Thailand in October.

'The teaching was the aspect of the trip that I was most worried about but, if anything, I was more unprepared for the disarming friendliness of the Karen people who I lived with for six months. I stayed with a family in a village near to the secondary school where I was teaching, and they took me in and treated me like a son and a brother. The way of life there is utterly different from what I'd become used to, in every way. Meals were simple but delicious, the shower was a bucket of water and the toilet was a hole in the ground. The thing that struck me the most was that the pace of life is so much more relaxed than at home in England. Often I didn't know what I'd be doing from one day to the next.

'I find it hard to remember what I thought my time in Thailand would be like when I originally boarded my flight at Heathrow so many months before. In any case, I had an amazing time there, and an unforgettable experience. The people I met, the things I've seen: nothing can take that away from me.'

Jo's profile

Raleigh International gave Jo Vellino one of her first chances of independence from her identical twin sister. They had done the same thing all their lives, so when Jo decided to take a gap year before going to university she was determined to do something on her own.

'I'd looked at a number of organisations, and most cost a lot of money, so I knew that I would have to earn some money. Raleigh costs £3000, but it organises some fundraising events, which helped. I did 'The Vertical Challenge': I had to persuade a team of five friends to walk up the stairs in Guy's Hospital Tower – 33 flights – until they had reached the equivalent of the height of Mount Everest! In fact I raised the money much earlier than I expected. I worked in a café for the entire summer, and ended up managing it – from 6am every day, six days a week!

'When I arrived there were about 100 of us in the group, all wearing Raleigh T-shirts. We were heading for Windhoek, capital of Namibia. We did three projects of three weeks each – an environmental project, a community project and a tracking project. With the odd day to move from one project to another, this makes a total of ten weeks. You are allocated to the projects, no choice, and you work with a different team each time. My first was the environmental project, which was on the Hoanib River, surveying a particular tree called the Anaboom that is the main source of food for elephants and giraffes. We had to measure the height of the tree, the width of the canopy, the state of the bark, any signs of wildlife and so on.

'The second project was a community project building a school, right in the north of Namibia, in a tiny village called

Mukundu. An earlier group had done the foundations and laid three rows of bricks; we carried on where they left off.

'We had a Raleigh builder who taught us for just one day how to do it! Members of staff supervised us, and we completed all the walls, exterior and interior for two classrooms with a store cupboard in between. Unlike the first project, we were based in one place. Our little camp was right in the middle of the village, which had 250 inhabitants. We had to put up a bramble fence to keep the local goats out, and usually had about 90 children watching everything we did! We did get the chance to get to know some of the locals – the adults would beg for lifts when we went into town, and we played football and had a sing-song with the kids.

'The final project took us up the Brandenberg Mountains. Here, research students from the University of Leeds School of Biology were investigating endemic lizards for the Namibian government. Our task was to catch the lizards with fishing rods – I was useless at it, so I always had to do the measuring! We also had to note any new species we found, and do tests such as flying a kite over their holes to see how they would react to birds.

'It was a huge learning curve, especially the first project. I think I was always very easy-going, but I'm even more tolerant now; I learned to respect other people, get along with them. We had to work with whoever else was assigned to our task. Sometimes, I felt very alone – my twin sister and all my friends were so far away. I learned to pick up a book and be content by myself. We met with a staff member at least once or twice on every project, and this gave us the chance to reflect on the learning, even though it was a casual chat.'

Rachel's profile

Rachel took a year off between Highers and her degree; she decided to take up the challenge of being a full-time volunteer with CSV.

'I had chosen a degree in social work but I needed experience to gain entry on to the course, so CSV was ideal. It appealed because the scheme places you away from home; I was itching to get out on my own, plus the fact that they try and place you in the line of work that most suits you and will be challenging. Also, they take volunteers at 17, the age at which we leave school in Scotland.

'I was placed on the Isle of Wight as a live-in carer for three adults with learning difficulties. My main duty was to watch over the day-to-day running of the house and to act as a support to them both physically and emotionally. I would escort residents to various activities such as bowling or swimming, help them with the shopping and to cook for themselves. I also had to live in the house with them and do what we called five 'sleep-ins' per week so that they had through-the-night care if needed. A couple of months into the placement I had to settle a new resident into the house, which was extremely complicated and stressful but a very good learning experience for me and my residents and a great confidence-booster. Two of the residents took part in activities with another charity and through them I got involved as well, which gave me a lot more experience and a wider outlook as I was working with both adults and children with learning difficulties and special needs.

'On my nights off I stayed at the flat that all the CSVs shared; there were seven of us on the island. We didn't have the same nights off but sometimes the flat would get a bit overrun. The flat was in Ryde, which is where I worked, so it was ideal for me if anything got a bit hectic. I could just pop up to the flat – someone was always there.

'It was a very trying time for me. In the beginning I didn't even know where the Isle of Wight was and I wasn't quite sure what my job would entail. It took quite a few weeks to settle in, but once I did I thoroughly enjoyed my work, even though it could be incredibly stressful and demanding at times. I think I matured a lot throughout this time and a lot of people commented on how I had changed. I became more independent, less temperamental and less selfish. I began to appreciate the comforts of home more and to put others before myself when it was needed. I hardened up a lot through my various experiences and found that I could tackle problems with a better understanding and maturity, But most of all, I saw life from a different perspective.'

Is voluntary work an option for you?

Many types of voluntary work are available, in your own home town, elsewhere in the UK or abroad. So, what's in it for you?

Why do voluntary work?	Why not?
it's your chance to give something back to society	while you will have money to live on, it won't be much
whatever you do, you are likely to feel that it is worthwhile, necessary and of benefit to others	you may be asked in advance to commit yourself for a set period of time
you may be able to gain work experience or personal skills that will be useful to your future career	some voluntary work can be physically or emotionally draining
you could decide to do voluntary work abroad and do some travelling as well	it could be difficult to save anything to fund your travel plans
you are likely to meet lots of people, and usually will work with others, so it's less likely you'll be lonely	you may have to live in basic accommodation

Committed on a voluntary project, even for a few weeks, with no means to get away, can be daunting. Is it for you? Try this quiz to help you decide.

The 'Voluntary Work – Can you Cope?' Quiz

1. You decide to stay at home for part of your gap year and do local voluntary work. Do you:

    a ask your local youth club if they need any help
    b contact your nearest volunteer bureau for ideas of which organisations need help locally

c using a directory that contains thousands of charities, contact lots of them and ask if there are any outlets near where you live?

2. You want to volunteer in the UK, but to live away from home. Do you:

    a decide which part of the country you want to live in and only look for opportunities in that area
    b search the Web, eg volunteering.org, and look for examples of volunteer work organisations in any area
    c get hold of a copy of *Voluntary Agencies Directory* from your local careers library and see which organisations appeal to you, and write to lots of them asking for their details and their support networks?

3. You see an advert for an organisation you've never heard of to work in return for bed and breakfast in Romania. Do you:

    a ask a friend who has done voluntary work in Africa if they have heard of it
    b contact the organisation for details and ask to speak to ex-volunteers from the project
    c read all the travel books you can find on Romania, then worry that the standard of accommodation provided may be basic?

4. Your granddad is ill just before you go. Do you:

    a check out the communication arrangements in the place you are going to and promise to keep in regular touch
    b check out any emergency repatriation arrangements with the organisation you are going with to confirm you could get home in an emergency
    c cancel your plans, just in case?

5. You want to do something different and take part in an environmental/scientific expedition. You have to pay £2800 to go. Do you:

    a forget it, you don't have that kind of money
    b ask the organisation for help with ideas on fundraising
    c plan a lot of small-scale fundraising events and after a while realise you are going to fall well short of your target?

How did you get on?

Mainly a: you don't devote enough time to preparation and planning, give up easily and make assumptions that may not be true. You need to question your chances of enjoying the experience.

Mainly b: you seem to show common sense and some persistence, both essential qualities for a volunteer.

Mainly c: you seem a little daunted by the idea – some types of project could suit you, but think carefully about how you would cope.

If you still think voluntary work is for you, now start some planning and preparation.

 Next step

For lists of the huge range of organisations involved with volunteering organisations, use the books and websites listed in Chapter 10 – Factfile. Particularly check out:

- **www.theyearoutgroup.org**
- **www.volunteering.org.uk (National Centre for Volunteering)**
- **www.worldwidevolunteering.org.uk (Worldwide Volunteering for Young People)**

---

5. Study

'I have been busy gaining sport coaching awards and experiences to help me further my career ambitions when I return.'

'I decided to learn Spanish early in my gap year, in preparation for a trip to Mexico later in the year.'

You can use your gap year to pick up a new skill through a short course. The range of courses is enormous, covering everything from computer skills to acupuncture. You can do courses through either the public or the private sector.

What do you need to consider when thinking about adding a course to your gap year?

Why do a short course?	Why not?
if you can't find a job, a course can help you structure your time and develop an interest	you may need to pay fees for courses
you may get a reduction in any course fees if you are unemployed	some courses are privately run, so you will need to seek them out and they can be expensive
completing a short course may make it easier for you to find temporary employment before and during a university course	if you are claiming benefits you'll need to check to make sure that the course does not exclude you from continuing to receive them
it shows that you're prepared to try something new or improve on existing skills	not all courses will lead to nationally recognised qualifications, so care is needed with selection
it can help keep your hand in re study and sitting exams	a course may only fill part of your time, so you'll need to consider what to do the rest of the time
if you study abroad, it's one way of spending time in another country	funding a course abroad can be costly
you can include a course abroad as part of your travel itinerary	applying for courses abroad can be time-consuming and requires a lot of effort to research

What courses can you do?

You could choose to do a course that teaches a practical skill, such as information technology, office skills, catering (or simply cooking), language study, arts and crafts, childcare, health, fitness and beauty, sports coaching.

Or you could attend college to pick up one or two more academic subjects. Some courses, such as business and IT, can help you get more lucrative temporary work in your gap year and beyond.

Your local further education college is likely to run a wide range of courses: full-time, part-time and distance learning courses. Private colleges may give you the opportunity to study courses that do not appear regularly in the public sector – such as riding instruction, cordon bleu cookery or complementary medicine.

Your other option would be to take a course by distance learning or online via e-learning, which would give you the opportunity of a more flexible learning programme. In this way you could combine work with study, which would help with finances. Look on www.ecctis.co.uk or www.learndirect.co.uk for details. What you pay depends on your status (ie whether you are working, looking for a job or in receipt of state benefits).

Teaching English as a Foreign Language (TEFL) courses are available both in the UK and abroad and can last from a weekend to a month. Some courses employ staff to help you get a job abroad afterwards. Typical four-week courses cost about £800–1000. Look at the book *Teaching English Abroad* for details.

Courses abroad

There are two main alternatives if you want to do a course abroad:

1. Take a degree or diploma course in this country that includes a term or a year abroad. This is fairly routine for those studying languages, but is also becoming a possibility for students of other subjects, including the sciences, engineering and humanities. The time abroad could be just to improve your language skills, or could be in another English-speaking country, where you continue to study your degree subject.

2. Organise a course independently before, during or after university. This is harder to arrange and to finance. You have to be prepared to do a lot of research, and planning ahead (up to two years in many cases) is essential. Language courses are often studied abroad as well as in the UK. Organisations such as CESA Languages Abroad or Council Exchanges run short courses for people over 16 in Europe and beyond. Shop around, as prices vary, eg a four-week Italian course in Florence with Council Exchanges costs £620 with accommodation.

 Next step

If you decide doing a course is going to be part of your gap year, follow up the information sources detailed in Chapter 10 – Factfile – and ask for help and advice from your careers or Connexions service.

---

6. Mixing it

Research with University of Birmingham students showed that the majority of students who took a gap year after university did a mixture of things. In the same research, 92 per cent of graduate employers in the study preferred that students did more than one activity during their gap year.

For example, one graduate in the study amazingly managed to cram the following into her 18-month gap:

- **nine months backpacking**
- **worked for the Department of Conservation in New Zealand in wildlife care for one month**
- **worked at a stockbrokers in Birmingham doing office administration**
- **worked for two months in New Zealand in office administration**
- **a safari in South Africa**
- **an expedition to Victoria Falls in Zimbabwe**

- **a three-day trek in New Zealand**
- **learned Spanish in preparation for a visit to Mexico.**

You may not be able to pack as many activities into your gap year, but it shows what is possible!

There are a number of plus points for mixing what you do, but be aware that if you don't plan and make decisions about how you are going to spend your time:

- **you risk drifting and ending up doing nothing in particular**
- **you could lose sight of your reasons for taking time out**
- **your CV could look a little empty for that year if you just 'messed about'**
- **you may find it harder to identify what you have gained from your experience, which is often the most valuable benefit of time out.**

Most of the young people featured in this book did several activities. In particular, look at Aruna's experiences and read Helen's account below.

Aruna (see her account in the Introduction) did care work in England, France, Romania and India (mainly with children and adults with severe learning and physical difficulties). Also while in France she did an intensive language course and worked in a model agency. She used her experiences in Romania to format a proposal for her dissertation and revisited the orphanage to carry this out. All this relevant experience will help her achieve her aim in becoming a clinical psychologist.

Helen's profile

Helen decided to take a year out after getting her first degree and before studying for an MA in Modern History.

'As it turned out I did a mixture of things during the year. Whilst waiting for my voluntary placement to be organised through CSV I had a temporary job in a prison on the switchboard. Although the work itself was not demanding I enjoyed dealing with a wide range of callers and the job gave me an insight into a new and rather unusual environment. I then spent six months as a volunteer, working as part of a team of carers for a severely disabled student. In order to do this I had to move to a completely different part of the country. This was followed by a period of bar work in a local holiday camp and then a backpacking trip to the US.

'But what did I get out of these varied experiences? My year out really increased my confidence. Up until then most of my achievements had been academic but now I feel that I can do an awful lot more and I can draw on positive examples from my year out. My time spent as a volunteer showed that I can adapt readily to new situations and people and take on a higher level of responsibility, in this case, ultimately for someone's life.

'I can also make a more informed decision about my future career as the variety of work I undertook helped me to discover what was important to me. I realise that I need contact with people as a major part of any future job, something I probably would not have done if I had simply stayed on to do the MA straight away, as I would have had nothing to compare it with.

'The time out has also helped me to live with uncertainty. I had a place on a course but I had to wait until my return from the US in August before I knew that I would receive a studentship from the Arts and Humanities Research Board. I was worried about whether or not I would be able to afford to do the course but I felt much more confident in my ability to adapt to a change in my plans should the money not be available.

'At first returning to study was difficult because of my time out. I did feel out of practice and basic student skills such as notetaking needed some revision but, on the other hand, I felt very motivated. I had, after all, made a conscious decision to complete the MA rather than drifting into it after finals. I was also more disciplined; I had been working long hours in my previous job so I found it fairly easy to organise my time effectively and still appreciate what university life could offer me.'

⤶ Next step

If you decide to include some of the options in this chapter as part of your year out, use the **checklists** in Chapter 10 – Factfile – to help you get started with your planning.

FAMILY FOCUS

4

It is a fact of life that parents worry. Their view of you is different from everyone else's. If you want to do a gap year it helps enormously to have them on your side.

Recent research suggests that the psychological support of parents is very important to those who have a gap year.[1] If something goes wrong they are your ultimate support. It is rare to find students who carry out their plans if their parents never warm to the idea.

They can help you weigh up the options, but on the other hand their opinions can be the opposite of yours. Either way you are likely to have to take their views into account, so try to get them on your side from the kick-off.

Have a look at some parents' experiences below to help you see things from their point of view.

---

[1] *Time Out: A study of the influences of postgraduation time out on career-decision making, entry into the employment market and career development.* Margaret Flynn (Careers Adviser, University of Birmingham). Dissertation for MA in Careers Guidance in Higher Education, University of Reading. March 2002.

Catering work in the UK and Europe

Parent's view

Clare Hurford's son Anthony had two periods of time out – before and after a course in environmental science at Leeds University. In his gap year before university he worked and travelled in Europe. After leaving university he went to Indonesia to teach English. Clare reflects on her view of gap years before university.

'My first experience of gap years was with my god-daughter, who went to work in France for a year before embarking on a languages degree. That year was followed by a year in Canada and when she finally returned to England to start her course she couldn't settle: she felt more mature and worldly-wise than the other students and her spoken French was already beyond degree level, so after a month she gave up and returned to the "real world" in Italy.

'When my son then planned to have a gap year I was aware that he might never return to studying. I had also listened to parents whose offspring had spent the year dossing at home or serving in the local burger bar, which I considered rather a waste of time unless there was a physical or psychological need just to chill out after the trauma of A levels.

'Going to university had been a very positive experience for me in that it distanced me from a strict Catholic upbringing and introduced me to a wide range of people and ideas that I had never encountered at school or home. Academically I floundered, as the course I had chosen was too difficult for me and I realised I had no interest in a biochemical career. The benefits for me then were exclusively social and emotional, thanks to the novelty of freedom and mixed, stimulating company.

'My son had enjoyed those freedoms already and didn't seem to have a clear idea of the career he wanted to pursue so I felt that a gap year would give him the challenge of surviving in a different environment without the pressures of studying. I was concerned about his safety and happiness but would not have been horrified if it made him rethink his future, even to the extent of rejecting university.

'Initially he worked in a burger bar near home but soon tired of the grease so fixed himself up with a "Job in the Alps". We were both apprehensive as we kissed goodbye on a dark December morning and for weeks afterwards I used to walk into his bedroom feeling sad and melancholy, but he was safe and happy in a hotel in Switzerland learning silver service and dressing up for the Christmas and New Year festivities. He rang regularly to report on his lessons on wine and cigars, the young people he met and the occasional British guests who were pleased to have a waiter who understood them. His German was improving and after New Year he was able to go skiing, sledging and snowboarding between shifts and was obviously enjoying the experience.

'At the end of his contract he bought a Rail Rover and went off with one of the other waiters for a month visiting Rome, Athens, Prague, Vienna and Amsterdam. When he returned he seemed more confident and sociable, had made several friends, some of whom are still in contact, and was still keen to start his degree in Leeds. He returned to the same hotel the following summer as a night porter and sounded like a native when I rang him one night. The travel bug was still alive in him after graduating so he acquired a TESOL certificate and taught English in Indonesia, then Switzerland, where he is now trying to decide what to do next!

'In some ways I could claim that the gap year unsettled him but he was never a placid or settled kind of boy. I think he adopted a brotherly role in his first year at university with the students, who were mostly younger than him, and he loves meeting and getting to know lots of people – perhaps the gap year was just a piece in the jigsaw of his adult personality. It's difficult advising other parents because everyone has different ideas about life and work. If you're intent on controlling your kids and their destiny it's going to be hard to let go and watch them wander off your map. I never had a map so it's easier for me to let him follow his instincts, which usually mean he's safe and happy, despite enjoying a high level of risk.'

Anthony's profile

Anthony reflects on his year out before university.

'I think my decision not to go straight into university life was based on a desire to do something different, and at that time unconventional, linked with my growing notion of working for a ski season and becoming an awesome skier! This seemed more realistic after finding a reference to the Jobs in the Alps in the careers library – a work agency that links people like me with the jobs they want. I applied to the agency and after a relaxed interview was offered a job. I had no real idea of what I would do after this season's work, but I figured something would work out.

'I don't think my parents played a big part in my decision to take a gap year, but I know they didn't try to put me off the idea. While I was away they lent support as familiar voices on the phone during the more testing times. My mum also helped by providing me with a BT chargecard, which I abused through keeping in touch with my girlfriend at the time – this landed me with a big bill on my return home, so I definitely learned a big financial lesson.

'Leaving home was a particularly emotional experience, but more because of what was ending than the exciting new beginning ahead. After all, I was to become a waiter in a four-star hotel restaurant! The first few weeks of the season are the most stressful because it's high season – Christmas and New Year and the hotel's full. I kept in touch with friends and family and scraped by. As the workload decreased days off became possible and my snowboarding skills blossomed, so things looked much brighter.

'I had such a wide variety of experiences that, more than anything, I developed a perspective of the world on which my life is largely based now – I'm working in Switzerland again and have been for the last 15 months. I met people from all over Europe, I improved my German ability immeasurably, I learned how to get by on my own in a number of foreign cities and survive on bread and cheese, I polished endless trays of cutlery with stinking hangovers and I tore down mountains with a snowboard strapped to my feet. People learn different things from different experiences. It's hard to say exactly what I learned because there's so much, but with such an intensity of experience you can't help but learn and grow.'

A ski season in Canada

Parent's view

Kathleen and Tony Jones's daughter Catherine also had a gap year before university.

'We experienced a variety of feelings when Catherine decided to take a year away from study between school and starting at university. One of her older brothers had travelled in Canada and Australia after finishing school five years previously, so we were not surprised when Catherine seriously considered a gap year as one of the options after school.

'There are some obvious concerns that spring readily to mind, such as the dangers of travel and work abroad, living in a different culture/environment, letting your child "go", the financial and health implications. However, most of these perceived concerns could be addressed through discussion and practical steps. They were also balanced against our feelings that such a time could be very beneficial. It is a time when there are hardly any responsibilities and possibly the only time when Catherine would be able to say "I'm collecting money before Christmas to spend after Christmas", without having to worry about the rent, tax, housing etc.

'It would be difficult to offer advice to other parents, as all situations are different. However, we did feel that it was necessary for Catherine to have a deferred place at university, as this provided a focus for the year and a definite reason to return. It is also important to be involved in the planning – ready to discuss details and to offer advice. We were pleased that Catherine chose BUNAC, thus giving herself a framework, a serious approach to an exciting experience and a means of contact in difficulties.

'Living and working away from home in a chosen environment was a positive experience for Catherine. The demands of the workplace had to be met, giving financial rewards for her effort. Her own leisure time was free from the usual responsibilities that come with regular employment and could be enjoyed with others of her own age. She became aware of her own background and how she was perceived by others and she was able to adapt to living with groups of people with different lifestyles and backgrounds. We also felt that some of the benefits were less tangible, and maybe in the long term the most important – the need to make her own decisions and live with the consequences, to be financially responsible, to use time effectively, to broaden her outlook by meeting people in different environments.

'Fortunately our obvious worries about safety, in all its aspects, were not realised. It had taken Catherine a good deal of thought to organise her year, having to make sure that she could manage the finances to make the commitment in the first place. Although she had a work permit she travelled to Canada without a job to go to. There was a great deal of uncertainty and we were concerned that she would be unhappy. In the event one of her most difficult situations was when, after a lot of job searching, she didn't know which of the three jobs she had been offered to take. We also learned that the things which need to be addressed are often those that have not been thought of, such as when Catherine was delayed for three days in Vancouver airport on her return because of a strike by the airline. It was then that we were so pleased that Catherine had kept in touch by telephone and letter and an emergency did not turn into a disaster.'

Catherine's profile

Catherine's view of the year confirms her parent's confidence.

'My parents were extremely supportive when it came to my taking a year out. My eldest brother had also taken a gap year and I think they saw the benefit of what he had done with his year out. I lived at home for the first part of the year so they were very involved with the whole organisation of my trip. Whilst I was away I always knew that they were on the other end of the phone line if I needed them and I could just come home if things didn't work out. This put my mind at rest and allowed me to enjoy myself knowing I had help if I needed it. My gap year also worked out quite well for my parents as they used it as an opportunity to visit me in Canada for a two-week holiday – no wonder they encouraged me to go!'

More detail on Catherine's gap year is in Chapter 3 – What Can I Do? – Work abroad.

Office and retail work in the UK and France

Parent's view

Penny's daughter Harriet decided to go to France and Spain for a year after her A levels.

'Early in Harriet's final A-level year she introduced the idea of taking a year out. She saw it as an opportunity to develop her language skills, and to become more independent in preparation for university. I was enthusiastic from the start but her father was more cautious. I saw the benefits for future employment, during or after university, and a means to ease the transition from school to the wider world of higher education.

'She decided to divide the year into three parts and work in London, France and Spain. She was interested in working in South America but unfortunately the GAP programme she wanted to do there was already full. In addition, her father was concerned about her working in South America so she compromised and decided on Spain instead. I admired the way she was able to make her own decisions whilst taking our views into account.

'I am sure that when she starts university to study French and Spanish she will be much better prepared academically and socially for her four-year course, especially for the year abroad.'

Harriet's profile

Harriet gives her view of the experience.

'As my birthday is in August I had always felt younger than my friends. And university seemed to be for older, mature people. This, added to the fact that I wanted to improve my languages, was the reason I decided to take a year out.

'Mum was all for it. I think she was trying to live the life she hadn't had, through me – she loves travelling and that culture stuff – whereas Dad was pretty wary. I think he was just scared of the insecurity of a year off and the extra year on top of a four-year degree course. In his mind it would have been easier and neater, in a way, to go straight from school to university. But, with advice from my teachers, I decided I wanted to do it.

'I knew that I didn't want to waste the year off, so I tried to plan it. As I'm going to study French and Spanish at university I thought it would be a good idea to spend some time in each country. But before doing that I decided to work in England for some experience and money. In the end I got jobs through contacts in London and Paris, which is where I am now. Spain is the next step – I'm hoping to travel around with a friend.

'Living independently has really been an eye-opener, especially in a foreign country. I have had to open a bank account and obtain a *carte de séjour* (residence card), both of which involve masses of French bureaucracy. Paying rent and bills is a new experience!

'Working was also new to me – before my gap year I never even had a Saturday job. Public relations in London was really interesting and a good introduction to the job world. I learned simple things like faxing and copying, but also how to deal with impatient journalists on the phone. I had a great time working in retail in Paris as there is so much variety to the work.

'Anyway, I am extremely happy with my decision and the way that the year is going, which makes it easier for Dad to accept it. And Mum can see how I've changed for the better over the past eight months. So far, the time out has been a success.'

Getting parents on your side

Support of your parents can be a big asset. So how can you get them on your side?

Parents' questions	Ideas you could use in reply
Why? What will you gain?	Be clear about your motivations for taking a year out. Parents will be more ready to listen rather than think 'It's just another whim!'
If you want to travel, will you come back alive and well? They have read news reports about the backpackers killed in the hostel fire in Australia in 2000 . . . and the girl who died in a lake in Africa . . .	Don't deny there are risks, but discuss the number of people who do a gap year compared with the small number who come to some harm. Show them the 'travelwithcare' website to suggest you do take safety seriously. Investigate insurance.
How will you keep in touch?	Investigate e-mail links. Tell them about Post Restante (through post offices). Agree regular contact.
Can you cope with the unexpected? They haven't forgotten the time when they had to help you out of a sticky situation a few years ago!	Think of examples in recent months where you have coped. If travelling is on your list suggest you go off for a couple of weeks as a trial run.
When you return, will you still want to go to university, or will you become a permanent drop-out?	A possibility. Is it likely? Tell them about the estimated 15 per cent who go to university having had a gap year.
Will you change too much? Parents often feel insecure about your going to university and growing away from them.	You're getting older. You will change anyway. It's normal. Give examples of people you know . . .

Parents' questions	Ideas you could use in reply
Do you know what to do in an emergency – will you panic?	Show them research you have done – embassy help/voluntary project safety nets.
What will it cost and will they need to pay anything?	Show them your budget notes.
What do admissions tutors think? Will it disadvantage your applying to university?	Show them notes from university open days – names of tutors and courses. Show them books such as this one or *Making the Most of your Gap Year*.
What about employers? Will they see you as unreliable and likely to quit and rush off again?	Point them to the research done on the topic and the Year Out Group website.

Some of these questions are the same as the ones you need to ask yourself – so doing some research will serve both purposes.

It's no good just saying 'I'll be fine. Stop fussing!' They will want EVIDENCE you have thought about it and are serious.

 Next step

Suggest your parents look at the 'parents' sections of the websites: www.gap-year.org.uk and www.gapyear.com.

TEACHERS' TIPS
5

If you are at school or college and considering a gap year before university, teaching staff will be very interested in what you plan to do next. Don't underestimate the help you can get from your teachers, some of whom may have done gap years themselves. They can:

- **advise you on any issues that are worrying you about your plans**
- **help with deferred entry and how to sell it on UCAS forms**
- **help with making applications during your gap year**
- **write references that positively reflect the effort you have put into planning the year.**

What do teachers think about taking time out?

Teachers from a range of schools and colleges offer their advice:

Sixth form college view

Student Services, Worcester Sixth Form College, suggest the following.

'Do take advantage of your teachers' and tutors' experience of working with students planning a gap year. We have many resources available, useful contacts with year out organisations and our own advisers who are ready and willing to help. We may even come up with suggestions you have not thought of! We also keep in touch with students who are taking a gap year and look forward to hearing about their experiences and feedback on organisations.'

Here are some further comments from the Head of Student Services.

'Even though we talk about a gap year to students at college, we need to help them realise the time can be made up of several short experiences. They do not have to commit themselves to a whole year of one type of experience with one employer or organisation. This can make the idea seem more manageable.

'There seem to be fewer students applying for deferred entry to university, especially if their AS results are disappointing. They want to wait and see if their A2 results are better than predicted, or they need more time to make up their minds. This is a good idea for some, but gaining a deferred entry place can give a goal to aim for and students can always withdraw and reapply the following year.'

Independent school view

Sally Billingham, from King Edward's School in Edgbaston, Birmingham (an independent, selective, boys' day school) has this to add.

'At King Edward's taking a gap year is discussed in Year 12 and, once research has been done (or not done!), about 15 per cent of the year group take a gap year. The choice of what to do varies greatly. The majority will choose to do their gap year with a recognised 'gap' organisation; others will make their own plans using contacts via family or friends. The school also has contacts with other schools in Australia and South Africa.

'Most wish to spend all or part of their year abroad. Some spend time abroad teaching English or doing care or environmental work. Organisations used for this type of work include The Gap Organisation and Teaching Projects Abroad. Venues have included New Zealand, Fiji, India, Nepal and Chile, to name but a few. A few students with a strong Christian background have had excellent placements with the Righthand Trust in Africa. They return from such years out with increased confidence and greater maturity and also a greater appreciation of their own standard of living and a real understanding of the needs of the third world.

'Those who plan to study engineering (or sometimes business studies or management) often choose to spend their year in the UK gaining experience through the Year in Industry scheme. At the end of this the transformation from sixth form student to confident young man is impressive! Another option for aspiring engineers is the Smallpeice Trust, which has an emphasis on improving a foreign language and spending time in a European manufacturing company.

'The school wholeheartedly supports the idea of a gap year. It not only allows the student a "breathing space" from his studies but provides time to mature and gain confidence and life experience. With so many students obtaining degrees today, it can often be the gap experience on the CV that makes the individual stand out from the crowd and get that initial interview and first job.'

Secondary school view

John McCall, Assistant Headteacher at Allerton Grange School, Leeds, shares his views and those of some of his colleagues.

'My first question is usually "Why?" Very often students will simply say that they fancy a break from studying. I feel that the school's role is to help them begin to think about how they can use the time effectively and to encourage them to look at the options available.

'Through taking a year out students also have an opportunity to reflect on the choices they have made. Some students follow a different degree path than they had originally considered. Some prefer to take a year off so they can apply for courses the year after they have left sixth form, safe in the knowledge of the grades they have achieved. This way they feel they are making a realistic choice of course and are not reliant on conditional offers.

'Staff may be able to suggest organisations that have helped students in the past to make the most of their year out, or even put pupils in contact with ex-students who have taken part in time-out activities. As part of our tutorial programme with Year 13 pupils we invite former students who have taken a year out to come back and talk about their experiences.

'We help students make their year out a selling point on their UCAS forms. They should always say what they want to do with the time and, very importantly, what they hope to gain. This not only makes it clear to an admissions tutor that the student has really thought about how they will use this time and putting together this personal statement can help students to focus on making the year out a successful experience. Staff can also help students by referring to their year out plans in the reference they write for the UCAS form, so that the universities are made aware of the school's approval of this course of action for the student.

'I have heard of (but never experienced) schools where students are discouraged from taking a year out because it doesn't look good on the "Pupil Destination Tables". If students feel their plans are not being met with any great enthusiasm they should try and find out what concerns the staff have. It may be that they are worried about a lack of commitment or structure to this proposed time out or are unsure how admissions tutors will react to a deferred application. If students still encounter problems, then the local careers service or Connexions is likely to be able to provide a range of information and help.

'If time out is well planned it can be a very beneficial experience. Sometimes, however, students don't always realise how much they've gained from their temporary job, travel or voluntary work. Thinking about how you've changed, the skills you've developed and the experience you've acquired is often the hardest part, but this is the type of information that future employers or admissions tutors are very interested in, and it can help students make future decisions about courses or careers. So keeping a travel diary, updating your CV or simply making a list of what you've gained from the year are all ways that you can make your experiences count.'

Applying for university/deferred entry

Teachers are experienced in dealing with university applications and can be a valuable source of advice for both deferred entry and applying in your gap year.

John Chester, Director of the Social Science Faculty at Cadbury Sixth Form College in Birmingham, is involved in UCAS applications and advises on the merits of applying for deferred entry, and offers tips if you decide to apply during your gap year.

'If you are planning to take a gap year between A levels and university it is usually advisable to apply at the "normal" time, ie in the autumn term of your A2/A-level year; and to apply for deferred entry – ie a year hence. I think this is usually the most sensible time to apply because:

- **Advice on courses, universities, completion of the UCAS form etc is readily available from your teachers and careers department, and university prospectuses and other resources will be easily accessible.**
- **Your school/college will be "geared up" to processing your application at this stage – your reference will be prepared and you will be on the school/college's system for electronic UCAS applications.**
- **Universities also regard this as the most convenient time to apply, and "deferred" applications are given equal treatment with applications for "immediate" entry.**
- **A gap year will involve less hassle if your university place is already secured.**

'If however you decide to make your university application during your gap year (because your estimated grades were too low for where you wanted to go, or you failed to gain a suitable place and preferred to reapply rather than go into Clearing etc), it is particularly important to:

- **apply as early as possible, eg before going abroad**
- **inform your school/college of your intention to apply, and if possible go in to discuss it with people who know you**
- **make sure that you provide an e-mail address if possible if you are going abroad**
- **failing that, make arrangements to keep in contact with a**

reliable person (usually a parent) who can deal on your behalf with communications from UCAS
• **be back in good time to make arrangements for university accommodation, finance etc.'**

For university admissions tutors' views on deferred entry see Chapter 6 – University/College Views.

Getting help from teachers

If you are still at school/college, you will probably spend quite a lot of time talking to the staff about what you plan to do when you leave. How are they likely to react when you suggest taking time out? Think about the questions they will ask you and have some responses ready.

Teachers' questions	Ideas to help with your replies
Why? What will you gain?	Refer to the lists you have made about your reasons for wanting a gap year.
Have you decided to apply for deferred entry to university or not? What are your reasons?	Think through your motivations.
What research have you done about university courses?	Prospectuses, websites, visits to universities.
Does your motivation at school/college show you can make a success of planning a year off?	Over to you!
Have you checked that tutors for the courses in which you are interested are willing to accept deferred entry?	Attend open days, do research on the Web, make direct contact with admissions tutors.

Teachers' questions	Ideas to help with your replies
Have you thought about how you will sell the idea on your UCAS form?	Draft a personal statement, and ask for advice.
Do you know what you need to do to apply during your gap year?	Find out how your school/ college can help once you have left.
What plans have you got for the year?	Read Chapter 3 – The Options – What Can I Do?, to get some ideas.
What research have you done into your ideas?	Use Chapter 10 – Factfile – at the end of this book to research your ideas further.
Have you used the resources available to you at school/ college?	Ask about the ways your school/college can help, eg is there relevant information in the library, have they contacts with past pupils who have done a gap year?
Have you any long-term career ideas? If so, what do these employers think of a year off?	Contact professional bodies of the careers in which you are interested or ask employers at careers fairs. Read Chapter 7 – Employers' Views.

UNIVERSITY/ COLLEGE VIEWS

6

The future in higher education

For many people taking time out before higher education is an obvious and attractive option. If you decide to apply for a deferred entry place at university during your final year at school or college you will be applying about 20 months in advance.

Changes in the way that applications are administered are currently being debated. It may help you decide when to apply for university (before or during your gap year) if you know what changes are being planned.

University admissions overview

Tony Higgins, Chief Executive of the Universities and Colleges Admissions Service, gives his views on what the future holds for higher education admissions.

'The first thing to say is that entry to higher education is bound to change enormously in the next ten years. The typical entrant will no longer be a full-time student offering high grades at A level. Because of changes in the methods of student financial support more students are likely to study part time rather than full time, or live at home. Others will move in and out of higher education as they earn the money to pay for their studies. Mature entrants will be able to use their work experience to gain credit for entry to courses at different levels.

'And the qualifications offered by school leavers will be different too: only a fifth of the young people that the government anticipates entering higher education in the future will have A levels. The new 16–19 curriculum arrangements now in schools and colleges will have a profound effect on the traditional young people's market.

'Universities are making courses more accessible by offering entry to people with work experience under the Credit Accumulation and Transfer Scheme. And they are offering places to students who do not have predicted grades in traditional qualifications such as A levels.

'A central clearing-house system will continue as the most efficient way of dealing with the needs of students and institutions. But there are many reasons why the procedures may change. At the moment, school leavers are having to commit themselves to a course of study at a time when their ideas and interests are changing rapidly. And because of the length of time between courses being listed and actually starting – some 20 months – students are often unaware of the up-to-date range of courses on offer.

'There is a strong argument for processing all applications after the examination results are known. Then all the applicants would be judged against the examination performance needed for entry. Students would be more mature – and more certain in their own minds of what they wanted to do. And the list of available courses would be up to date.

'There is clearly no opportunity to do this within the current timetable, but a restructuring of the HE academic year might enable students to start courses at more suitable times or to enter at two points in the year. In fairness, I think it is unlikely that the traditional start to the academic year in September/October is likely to change because of international collaboration, but a second entry point could well be flexible. Another alternative that has been discussed is a six-term school year that would enable students to take exams earlier (before hay-fever time) so that there might be longer (and sufficient) time between the publication of results and the start of the academic year to enable the full application process to be conducted after results are known. The Local Government Association appointed an independent Review Group to examine the structure of the school year and its recommendations for a six-term school year are receiving widespread support.

'The students entering higher education in the future will present different challenges to the admissions process. So it will have to respond to change.'

To help you decide whether to apply for deferred entry or to wait and apply for a place during your gap year – once you have your results – read the university admissions tutors' views below.

What do university admissions tutors think of deferred entry and gap years?

University attitudes to deferred entry vary. Some universities are very keen on gap years, for example, the 2003 University of Birmingham prospectus states:

> You may be thinking about deferring coming to Birmingham for a year in order to broaden your experience by working, travel, voluntary service or some other activity. We are happy for you to do this. If we are willing to offer you a place we will, in all cases, be willing to delay your entry for a year.

The Director of Admissions, Delyth Chambers, confirms:

'The University of Birmingham recognises the value of a gap year in encouraging students to become independent and self-sufficient and to develop skills that will be of use to them when they join a university. Students who have taken a gap year tend to be more mature and have few problems in settling into university life. There is also the added bonus of extra cash if the student has managed to work during their gap year, and generally a broader outlook on life. If someone has the opportunity to take a gap year I would really recommend it.'

David Hadley, Admissions Tutor for Environmental Management at the University of Birmingham, adds:

'Generally I feel gap years are a good thing to do. On the UCAS application form I ideally like to see work or some kind of experience related to the degree course they want to study, but it isn't essential. Students who have done a gap year seem to be more mature and have a better idea of their reasons for doing a degree. I have had some gap year students who take some time to get back into the habit of studying, but once they do this they settle in well.'

At University College Worcester, a smaller institution but one with a wide range of degree courses on offer, Martin Willis, Admissions Tutor for English, gives his view:

'On UCAS personal statements I like to see some indication of what is planned for the year, but I have no preconceptions about the activities undertaken. Some students need to do a gap year for financial reasons, and choose to work and save for a year. This can show dedication and a sense of forward planning.

'I have no preference whether students apply in Year 13 and ask to defer, or apply during their gap year. What is important is that they want to study English here at Worcester.

'When they arrive gap year students can sometimes feel a little out of touch with a structured education system, and it can take a bit of time to get back into it. This is usually just a short-term feeling, and the students are soon into the swing of student life!'

More points to consider . . .

Admissions tutors vary in what they prefer students to include as part of their gap year (eg for music they may ask you to keep up your level of performance). For most subjects admissions staff have no preference, but expect you to explain what you hope to gain from the experience.

At a few universities admissions staff may be less keen to offer deferred entry, so always ask for details before applying. In particular, check out music, medicine and maths courses. You may find that some courses will not accept deferred entry, but other universities offering the subject will.

For certain courses, especially at postgraduate level, some kind of relevant experience as part of a gap year is necessary. Social work postgraduate courses, for example, require at least nine months' experience in a caring environment (voluntary or paid), in addition to a degree, before you can be admitted to the course.

To summarise:

Why apply for deferred entry?	Why not wait?
some organised gap year schemes, eg BUNAC, require you to have a deferred entry place before accepting you for the scheme	you have more time to make up your mind about whether to go to university at all and choose the right course/university for you
you can concentrate on enjoying your gap year, knowing you have a place	after your gap year you may be less keen on your chosen course, start and find you are unhappy and want to change course
if you change your mind you can withdraw and	you have your results and can apply, confident you
reapply for another course in the future	meet the academic criteria for the course
you are applying whilst you	

Why apply for deferred entry?	Why not wait?
have the close support of teachers at school/college

if abroad, you may not be available for decisions and will need to rely on parents for issues such as applying for accommodation

You may have problems attending interviews if you are abroad or working; not all courses interview applicants, but many do | |

Convincing admissions tutors

When you come to apply for a university place, how are you going to convince admissions tutors that your gap year is a good idea?

University tutors are hoping to fill their courses when they interview you, whether you are applying for a first degree after school/college or a postgraduate course after completing your degree. They are looking for motivated students who will perform well on their course. Think about what they will be looking for on application forms or at interview.

University admissions tutors' questions	Ideas to help with your replies
What are your plans for the year?	Examples of alternative itineraries show your commitment to making best use of the year.
What will you gain from the gap year?	Be ready to explain your motivations and your choices.

University admissions tutors' questions	Ideas to help with your replies
Will your motivation to do their course remain high after a year out?	Produce examples of evidence of your interest in their subject.
If you have any career in mind after the course, will it help you achieve those aims?	Point to research you have done on any careers you are considering.
Have you got the practicalities sorted out, eg who will choose your accommodation?	Show you have thought about such issues in advance.
Will it mean you will perform better on their course when you return?	Stress which skills you think you will gain – extra confidence, initiative, maturity . . .
What will you do to make sure you have not forgotten the basic knowledge you will need on the course?	Look at ways you can keep your knowledge up to scratch, eg revision courses.
Will your plans give you experience directly relevant to the course?	If possible, try to include some relevant activities in your year.

 Next step

To help you decide whether to apply for deferred entry or not you will need more information. You could:

- **talk to teachers and see Chapter 5 – Teachers' Tips**
- **contact universities direct for details of their policy**
- **ask direct questions at open days to subject admissions tutors. These are the people who will be reading UCAS forms and making offers**
- **ask questions online via university websites, or at pre-planned 'virtual' open days (see www.studentUK.com).**

EMPLOYERS' VIEWS

7

At some point in the future it's likely that you will need to earn a living. So you need to take into account employers' views about gap years when making your plans, even though you may not be applying for jobs for several years.

In this chapter you can read the views of different types of employer, including the public sector (Civil Service), a major financial company, car manufacturer and a small public relations consultancy.

Employers' overview

Carl Gilleard, the Chief Executive of the **Association of Graduate Recruiters** (AGR), which represents 600 organisations that employ graduates, and who has been involved with research into gap years, gives an overview.

'We live in a time when "added value" matters. Employers seeking new recruits, especially those at the start of their working lives, look for candidates who offer something extra. Taking a year off and putting it to good use is one way of gaining additional skills and experiences that can add value in the workplace. So it has to be a good thing to do. It also helps to make an application for a job stand out and that can't be a bad thing either with the level of competition that is around for the best jobs.

'Regardless of whether time off is taken after A levels or after a degree, the essential requirement is to make good use of the year off. Make sure you plan it, make the most of the opportunities that present themselves, maximise the gains and enjoy it!

'At an interview you can then explain how you gained from the experience – flexibility, adaptability and resourcefulness. These are all qualities that employers look for in candidates. Perhaps the one thing all employers will frown upon is a sense that the year simply drifted by without any real progress or learning taking place.

'Virtually all work experience is good work experience, but a sandwich placement is usually related to the degree course and, quite possibly, the chosen career area. Therefore it should be directly relevant and structured accordingly. This will impress some employers. AGR's own survey shows that employers pay a premium to graduates who can offer "relevant work experience" and interestingly that premium amounts to more than that offered for a first-class honours degree.'

Does the attitude to a year off vary with the sort of employer and type of jobs they offer? Here are comments from companies in the commercial sector, public sector and manufacturing industries.

Commercial employer's view

Dr Andrew Bottomley, Head of Graduate Recruitment Marketing at **PricewaterhouseCoopers**, the largest private sector employer of graduates, comments as follows.

'A year off can provide strong evidence that helps differentiate an applicant from the rest of their peer group. What they have done with their year off is critical. Candidates who achieve little with their time will find employers looking sceptically at the gap in the application. By contrast, those who have structured their time and taken on challenges they would not normally have the opportunity to face come out of their year stronger people, with the attributes of initiative, motivation and commitment that we look for.

'Taking time out is equally valid for either A-level or post-degree students. Within our selection process we would certainly seek to gain information on the time spent during the year out and what the students feel they have gained from their diverse experiences. This will be the case regardless of whether the time was taken before or after degree-level studies.

'Interviewers will want to hear about what has been learned from the time out and not that the year was "good", "fine" or "OK". There is little possibility that everything went completely smoothly or that the entire year can only be described as "interesting". The year out is a learning experience, and the candidate needs to show self-awareness, demonstrating reflective learning of the skills that they have gained from the situations they have faced and how these may be applied in the future.

'It is also critical that students manage to show that they have been creative with their time out and that they have not just let the year pass them by.

'At interview each person is assessed against a set of core criteria: competencies and motivations derived from the business and current employees who are successful in their roles. These criteria cover everything from commercial awareness through to interpersonal skills and the ability to take initiatives. Interviewers must be able to gain evidence against each of these attributes and never make value judgements. A year out often gives candidates the opportunity to demonstrate and develop these talents and gives us a greater insight into their personality than can sometimes be achieved if the route has been straight through the education system.

'Any work experience gives students the opportunity to broaden their skills base, and whereas relevant work experience is the most useful, any experience will allow a job candidate to demonstrate how they coped with work-based situations and dealt with working alongside a range of staff.'

Small employer's view

Shirley Muir, Managing Director of the Aberdeen office of UK public relations consultancy **Beattie Media**, has developed and managed corporate communications programmes in several major UK companies and in public relations consultancies in the UK, US and Europe. She gives the view of a small employer, a consultancy with only five employees, working in the communications industry.

'There are a large number of corporate communications and media studies graduates on the job market today. There are also many graduates in other disciplines who are keen to break into the public relations business. As a result, competition is stiff for young people wanting to start a career in public relations or corporate communications. A small employer will select the candidate who can join the organisation and make a sound business contribution at a very early stage.

'Most young people have to be trained to perform even the most basic business functions when they are embarking on their first job, and this requires a big investment in time, a considerable burden for a small business. A new employee who can use initiative, who knows when to come for advice, when to work independently, and who rapidly fits into team working, will succeed. Of course the candidate must have the interview skills to "sell" his or her maturity and commitment to the interviewer. We would expect the candidate to explain why they embarked on a gap year away from formal education, what they hoped to achieve by it, what they actually achieved and can therefore offer as a bonus to an employer. They should be able to compare their own CV with that of a non-gap year competitor and explain why I should take them into my firm rather than the competitor.

'Any graduate who has taken a year out of education should be more self-reliant, a better team player, and should recognise how they have developed as an individual. That development can come as the result of a university work placement programme as part of their degree (very valuable to small employers), or working to build up funds during a gap year.

'Gap years are not always viewed with enthusiasm by employers. There is sometimes a suspicion that the gap year was an indulgence on the part of the parents to "buy" some competitive advantage, or even to buy them time to grow up a bit – especially in Scotland where youngsters leave school a year younger than in England and Wales.'

Public sector employer's view

After a career in the diplomatic service Graham Wilkinson now runs a recruitment and training consultancy that works with a number of central government departments. He gives a view of a public sector employer.

'From my perspective, based on extensive experience of graduate selection during the last 15 years, candidates who have taken a year off have distinct advantages when applying for public sector jobs (whether the year off is between school and university, or after graduating, is equally valid).

'The advantages lie in the fact that, whereas years ago most graduates joined the **Civil Service** straight after a first degree and were given extensive on-the-job training, nowadays most entrants are somewhat older and are expected to demonstrate during the selection process the qualities and competencies required for their first post. These include skills and abilities that are more likely to be developed (or expanded) during a year off than when the candidates are studying full time:

- **They have to be good communicators, comfortable with colleagues and "customers" (the public) from a variety of social and cultural backgrounds. In today's interdependent world graduates in public sector posts may find there is an international context to this role. Experience gained living, working or travelling abroad will be a positive asset during the selection process, providing the candidate is able to reflect thoughtfully upon, and learn from, their experiences.**
- **Candidates are also expected to demonstrate "managerial potential"; selectors will value extracurricular activities and school- or university-based organisational/leadership roles. However, workplace experience will be regarded more highly – a gap year in an industrial placement, or a period of structured work at home or abroad, whether paid or as a volunteer, will often furnish the applicant with relevant experience to discuss at interview.**
- **More generally, for many people the experience gained during a year off will have a maturing and broadening effect; candidates will be more self-confident, better able**

to make decisions and, often, more certain about their objectives. These characteristics can enable them to demonstrate the commitment and determination that selectors value so highly.'

Manufacturing employer's view

Ford, a major global automobile manufacturer, recruits graduates into a range of jobs including engineering, human resources, finance, IT, marketing and sales, purchasing and product development. Emma-Jane Finlay, Graduate Recruitment Supervisor, discusses **Ford**'s attitudes to gap years.

'We will welcome applications from people who have had a gap year. This applies whether they have had a gap year before university or afterwards. The fact that students have gone and done something such as take a gap year can help make them a more rounded individual. They would have a great range of experiences and opportunities to develop some key competencies that we are looking for. Any kind of activities are fine, but doing relevant work experience can impact on the level and salary at which they enter the company, the same as doing a year in industry whilst at university.

'At interview we look for exactly the same qualities from those who have done a gap year as from those who have not; the difference is that students who have taken a year off tend to have identified more examples that they can use to demonstrate key competencies.

'For those who have graduated, we do not advertise that we offer deferred entry, but if a candidate wishes to travel before they start with us they need to return the contract with an attached letter stating that this is the case. We can not guarantee that we will have places next year – as we do not have confirmed hiring numbers – but we will get in touch with them before we start the following year's recruitment campaign to offer them a place if possible.'

Employer research

In the last few years research has been conducted into employers' attitudes about taking a year off and about work experience. The results of the research show that employers agree on the benefits of time out, but add conditions to their approval.

Time well spent – research views

Research done in 2000 by Community Service Volunteers in association with the Association of Graduate Recruiters,[1] shows that 100 per cent of the employers who took part in the survey agreed that a constructive gap year helps to prepare people for the workplace. Of the participants, 88 per cent agreed that it equips graduates with skills such as initiative, communication, problem solving, decision making, teamworking and relationship building. The employers consulted were members of the Association of Graduate Recruiters.

Time out – research views

Research with University of Birmingham students[2] conducted in 2001 showed that employers are generally positive in recognising the benefits of taking a gap year. However, they look for evidence that the time has been spent constructively and expect graduates to identify the skills gained from their experiences.

'The study included a range of employers who advertise with the University of Birmingham Careers Centre for graduates to enter a wide range of job functions in their organisations. The

---

[1] *Time Well Spent*. Community Service Volunteers and Association of Graduate Recruiters. August 2000.

[2] *Time Out: A study of the influences of postgraduation time out on career-decision making, entry into the employment market and career development*. Margaret Flynn (Careers Adviser, University of Birmingham). Dissertation for MA in Careers Guidance in Higher Education, University of Reading. March 2002.

most interesting point from the study is the overwhelming support of employers for the skills and maturity benefits of taking time out. Larger employers and those with more flexible recruitment procedures were more likely to show a positive response.

'Employers were very clear in adding conditions to this approval. Time should be spent constructively and the graduates able to identify the skills gained from their experiences. All the respondents preferred a mix of activities done during the period of time out, with work experience in the UK or abroad heading their list.

'Employers were mainly neutral about the idea of taking more than one gap year – both prior to university and a period of time out afterwards – but several indicated they would want to see "very good reasons" for the second period of time out.

'Well over half of the respondents would consider offering deferred entry to candidates, but in reality information gathered from graduates returning from time out shows that very few actually managed to achieve an offer.'

Graduates' work – research views

Professor Lee Harvey is the Director of the Centre of Research into Quality at the University of Central England in Birmingham. He has undertaken an extensive study of the attributes that graduates will need in order to be successful at work in the 21st century.[3] One of the key findings is that employers and higher education institutions should be encouraged to provide work experience of some kind as an option on all courses. This was seen as the single most significant element by employers in both large and small companies. He has also done a follow-up study to the original report in 2002 and comments as follows.

'What employers are looking for these days are people who are bright, who have a range of attributes apart from subject

---

[3] *Graduates' Work: Organisational change and students' attributes.* Lee Harvey, Sue Moon and Vicki Geall, Centre for Research into Quality, University of Central England in Birmingham. 1997.

knowledge – the ability to work in teams, to communicate well, good interpersonal skills, who are flexible and can quickly adapt to the work culture. Usually they told us that people who had taken a year out were much better at doing that than those who had gone straight through the educational system.

'The majority of employers were happy for any kind of experience, good or bad, provided that the students could identify what they have gained. Some employers are looking for "relevant" experience but there are an equal number who are not. For example, one large law firm was looking particularly for people who had not spent all their time out working voluntarily in legal advice centres but who had gone round the world or erected circus tents or whatever. They were looking for something that showed the student could show initiative and operate in a less rarefied atmosphere, in a variety of everyday settings.

'Young people taking a year off, either before university or after they have graduated, should remember that it is going to be important to be able to talk about what they gained. Recruiters, on hearing that you have backpacked round the world, will not be interested in where you have been, but what you have learned.'

What can you do to make yourself attractive to employers?

If you are considering a year out after university applying for jobs could be just one step away. In making decisions about what to do in your gap year you have to take account of many different views (parents, teachers, admissions tutors), but at the end of the day it is employers who will be paying your salary. What they see on your CV influences whether they bother to interview you or not.

So, having read the views of a wide range of employers, how can you make yourself more attractive to them? Try to put yourself in their position and produce some convincing answers to employers' main concerns about a year off, whether it is on a CV, an application form or at interview.

Employers' questions	Ideas to help with your replies
What have you gained?	List the skills and qualities you think you have gained.
Have you done any experience relevant to the kind of work we do?	A plus point, even if you have just spent a few days doing unpaid work experience.
Are you able to articulate what you have learned from both good and bad experiences during the time out?	Think of some specific examples of situations you had to cope with.
Are you a 'gap year bore' and give too much detail of what you have done?	Think about your experiences and interpret only the relevant parts to the employer.
Have you used the time to help focus on the career you want?	Make use of help available, eg from your university careers service, attending employer fairs etc.
Are the skills you have gained relevant to the jobs we have to offer?	Research what the employer is looking for in detail.

IS IT ALL FOR ME?

8

Pulling it all together

Feeling confused by all this? You knew that people would have different reactions, but . . . It might help to bear in mind some of the following issues when putting your case to parents, teachers, university tutors, potential employers and, most importantly, yourself.

Parents

Parents usually have a great deal of influence on your plans between A levels and higher education. Even after graduation the chances are that they will be very interested in what you do and have their own opinions on what would be best. They are the people who know you best and their views are worth taking into account.

Teachers

If you are still at school/college, you will probably spend quite a lot of time talking to the staff about what you plan to do when you leave. How are they likely to react when you suggest taking time out? Think about the questions they will ask you and have some responses ready.

University tutors

University tutors, whether you are applying for a first degree after school/college or a postgraduate course once you have got your first degree, are hoping to fill their courses when they interview you. They are looking for motivated students who will perform well on their course.

Employers

For those considering a year out after university applying for jobs could be just one step away. While parents have their opinions, and tutors decide whether you get a place on their courses, it is employers who will ultimately pay your salary. What they see on a CV influences whether they bother to interview you or not.

What will their main concerns be?	
Parents	Teachers
• Your safety and happiness.	• Are you going to use the the time effectively and have you really thought about the pros and cons?
• Whether your choice for time out is likely to benefit either your study or your future career.	• Are you going to apply for deferred entry to university or need their help during your year off?
• Whether you have made sensible plans or are likely to waste your time.	
• Are you able to finance yourself, will you be earning, have you enough money to travel or might they have to contribute?	

What will their main concerns be?	
Employers	University admissions tutors
• How good are you likely to be at the work they require from you? How will your year help out with this?	• Will a year off affect your motivation to come on the course?
• What have you gained in terms of skills and personal qualities?	• Will your knowledge still be current enough to do the course?
• Have you done something positive with your year out and not just drifted through it?	• Will you settle into university life?
• Was any of your time spent gaining work experience?	• Will your experiences be advantageous to you whilst doing the course and when you leave and start a career?

So, what about you?

Are you persuaded a year off is the right thing for you? It may be easier to convince others if you think through where you are with your life and career plans generally.

Which describes your present position best?

A. I am certain I know what course/job I want after my time out.
B. I think I know the broad general area of work or study I am aiming for.
C. I haven't a clue what I want to do in the long term; perhaps time out will help me to decide.

Your answer	Points to consider
Answered A? . . . and are coming back to go on a course	• **What do you think your tutor's reaction will be to you taking time out? If you don't know, write and ask for an informal discussion to check over views and get advice on the best form of experience to acquire.** • **Why do you think your time out might help you to gain more from this course?** • **Have you applied for your course yet? If not, why not get the interviews out of the way now and see if you can defer entry?**
Answered A? . . . and are coming back to apply for jobs	• **Is there any chance of deferring a firm offer of employment? Have you tried? If this isn't possible, do you know how this particular occupation recruits? Are there lots of vacancies throughout the year, or will you have to be careful not to miss a closing date? If you don't know this check it out with your careers service, or with the appropriate company/professional body.** • **How will you explain how your time off will enhance what you can offer as an employee?** • **You may have to be prepared for more than one 'year off'. If you can't enter employment immediately after your return, how will you spend your time?**

Answered B?	• What experience will your time out give you that may help you to decide that your tentative interests are right for you? • In what ways will your time out help you to learn about yourself? A clearer view of your skills, values and interests will help when looking at the career areas you are exploring. • For how long can you afford to defer a decision? If you are not sure check closing dates for applications, or the usual job recruitment procedures, either direct or through your careers service.

Answered C?	• List all the options you are considering. Look at each in turn and decide what you will gain. What skills will you gain from each activity? • Are there any particular skills you want to develop, eg thinking on your feet, working in a team? • Who could you contact to talk through your ideas and relate them to possible future career choices?

If you have found answers to most of the above questions then you are likely to be more convincing in persuading people that you are doing the right thing – and in reassuring yourself too!

Add in your personal values

Looking at what you will gain from time out is only part of the picture. How important are the following in your life at the moment? Tick the five most important to you:

- ☐ having fun
- ☐ saving money
- ☐ meeting new people
- ☐ gaining qualifications
- ☐ learning a new skill (specify what)
- ☐ gaining confidence in yourself
- ☐ feeling secure
- ☐ having status
- ☐ building on relationships that are already important to you
- ☐ taking risks
- ☐ being envied
- ☐ seeing a clear outcome to your actions
- ☐ feeling that you have control over your life
- ☐ any other issues important to you (list them).

Think about your plans for the year – do they match up with your top five values?

Is it for me?

Having taken account of a range of experiences and views, and looked at all the options, in the end the decision is yours. Are you sold on the idea? If so it's time to start making some more definite plans.

 Next step

Describe in as much detail as possible what your time out will involve. Think about your immediate plans. Identify all the references that may be helpful. (See Chapter 10 – Factfile.) Use them to help you answer the following:

- **How much money will I need? Use the budgeting section of the gapyear.com website to help.**
- **How will I obtain this – and, if borrowing, how/when will I pay it back?**

- **Who do I need to contact to make arrangements?**
- **By when?**
- **What contingency plans have I made if things go wrong?**

Contingency plans

Many people on a gap year find that their plans need to change as time goes on. Flexibility is key, as even the most well-planned year may contain a few surprises and changes. Being flexible can form part of your contingency plans, so if you are working abroad and find that the cost of living is higher than you had budgeted for, or you can't get the job you wanted, you need to have some alternative plans ready for when you come back home.

Still concerned about what to do if things don't work out? This is the most common worry students have when thinking of a year out, so you aren't the only one!

The different chapters in this book are full of tips of how to plan, which is the main way to avoid getting into difficult situations. Chapters especially useful are:

- **Chapter 3 – What Can I Do? – for ideas of what to do if things go wrong.**
- **Chapter 10 – Factfile.**

Other good sources are: *Before You Go* by Tom Griffiths and the Gap Year website (www.gapyear.com).

You should minimise your problems if you:

- **have good insurance**
- **keep in touch with family and friends**
- **make sure you know how to get access to emergency money**
- **have copies of documents and numbers and think about where you keep the originals at all times**
- **look after your health**
- **read widely about the areas you plan to visit and the activities you plan to do**

- **take advice from others – teachers, parents and advisers, but also those who have been and done it!**

Clare Hurford, featured in Chapter 4 – Family Focus – gives her advice as a parent:

> 'My advice to parents is to do everything you can to make sure that your son or daughter has adequate insurance, any injections or medicines they need and an e-mail address. Then trust them to survive and enjoy their experience. Accidents do happen but the most likely outcome is that they will return safely, more appreciative of the home comforts they used to take for granted and keen to continue their studies.'

There will always be occasions when all the planning in the world won't have helped. Then your own resourcefulness is your best back-up. The trick is to always have alternative plans and be prepared to be flexible.

Still not sure? If you are still undecided, see how some students resolved some of their concerns in the . . .

Taking a year off chatroom

Applying to university . . .

Sophie – I decided to take a year out to decide what degree to do but I now find that time is passing me by and it's already October and I've not come to any decisions. If I don't apply for university soon I'll have missed out on next year too. I'm so muddled I don't know what to do for the best. Should I just apply for any course to make sure I get in?

Suki – What's the rush? A year out is a good time to take stock of your future plans but many people take two or even three years out before they decide to go to university. If you need longer to make up your mind then take longer. When I decided to postpone making my mind up about higher education my parents urged me at least to use my time positively. It was good advice – if you haven't found a job yet then start looking or, if you want to travel, start making plans. Taking time out is fine as long as you don't drift for too long.

Raj – I can't stand the thought of being a poverty-stricken student for three or four years, so I'd like to work before going to college. Can I apply and get a place and then leave it a year or two before taking it up?

Maria – I did just that! I decided to work for a couple of years and then go to university. I found a job that gave me some really good work experience which has helped me find vacation work now I am at uni. The money I was earning came in useful too as I was able to save quite a bit towards my tuition fees and living expenses. I enjoyed having some spare cash as well and it was quite tempting to stay in my job. I realised, however, that I really wanted to spend more time studying and was probably more motivated when I did start my course than I would have been after A levels.

Sam – Can I join in? Don't forget that you can usually only defer a place for one year. The admissions tutor for my course was all for me deferring and I've managed to find some voluntary work that relates to the degree I'm going to do. A friend of mine, however, had to be very persuasive. It's useful to think out your arguments in advance of filling out your application in case you have an interview.

Travelling alone . . .

Lucy – I want to take time out to travel, but my family say I'm nuts. They say a girl shouldn't travel alone as it's too risky. I think I'm pretty resourceful; has anyone out there ideas about how I can persuade them?

Ali – Hi, Lucy. I found it really helpful to find lots of examples in various books of girls who had travelled on their own and not only survived but thoroughly enjoyed their trip. I know that my Mum also felt happier when she saw how much research I was doing and books such as Lonely Planet guides do provide advice for single women travellers.

Jane – Hello, Lucy. My parents were very concerned about my plans of travelling on my own. I thought that I might never get beyond Dover! In the end they were much happier when I found a travelling companion through a family friend and even made a donation to my funds.

Applying for jobs . . . will employers want me?

Jess – Is there anyone out there? I'd like to take a year off after I graduate to help me decide what to do in the future. But I am not sure how employers will view this when I go for interviews later.

Jo – I saw your message and felt that I had to reply. Don't kid yourself that taking a year off after your degree will, in itself, help you sort out your career plans. I've seen one or two of my friends travel and work abroad for a while hoping that career ideas would simply pop into their heads, but when they came back to the UK they were still directionless. It may sound very obvious but you do need to put some work into thinking about the future rather than just letting it happen. Think about your skills, interests and abilities, find out about the graduate employment situation, and follow up any career ideas, however vague. It is far easier to do some research before you go, and you may be able to talk through some ideas with your careers adviser as well.

Jess – Thanks for the input. I'm still worried that employers might want me to get some management experience during my year out – I'm planning to work in the US for a few months and then travel. Is this the type of activity that would still interest employers?

Jo – You don't have to get a management job during your time out! You can learn a great deal from living and working in a different country. The really important thing is to convince employers that you have spent your time wisely and have gained something from it. Most graduate recruiters are looking for qualities such as time management, teamwork, communication skills, budgeting abilities – I made sure I gave myself chances to develop some of these skills whilst abroad and also I thought carefully about how I described my year out on application forms and at interview.

Coming back . . .

Jack – I feel like taking a year off and never coming back. I worked very hard for my degree but now can't find a decent job. I really wish I hadn't gone to university.

Pip – I know how you feel, Jack! It's a pretty demoralising experience to find that employers aren't queuing up to make use of your hard-won qualification. I planned to 'get away from it all' and thought that this would make things better but my sister pointed out that running away wasn't going to help.

Jack – It's good to know I'm not alone but that doesn't solve my problem. I'm willing to do anything and nobody seems interested.

Pip – Well, perhaps that's the problem. You don't sound too clear about which type of work would suit your skills and abilities. No employer wants a graduate who is just looking for any job. Spend a bit of time using your careers service (find out if there is any additional help available through Jobcentre Plus) and clarify your long-term plans. I had access to the Internet and found a good website – www.prospects.ac.uk – that had lots of information to help me plan my future.

Sally – I've just come into the chatroom and wanted to share my experience. I found it very useful to draw up a list of qualities that would particularly appeal to the kind of employer I was interested in and THEN I planned to use any time available to gain relevant voluntary work experience. Friends of mine have also taken short courses that gave them relevant skills (in computing or languages). My brother decided to backpack around Asia to build up his confidence and maturity. Good luck – although my Dad says that luck is when preparation and opportunity coincide!

Harry – I need help! After I got my degree I decided to take time off to do some travelling and broaden my experience. Everybody told me that this was a good idea – employers are really interested in graduates who have gained some maturity, and have got rid of the 'travel bug'. They were wrong! Since I came back to the UK I've written literally hundreds of applications – I'm prepared to do absolutely anything.

Sky – Don't panic, Harry. I felt the same when I came back from a great time in New Zealand. Employers just didn't seem to want to interview me, let alone offer me a job. People who told you that employers ARE interested in experience and maturity gained during time out are absolutely RIGHT – but you have to know how to talk about it! I spent too long just applying for every job that I was vaguely qualified for (and some for which I was not) until my friend pointed out that no employer is looking for candidates who want 'just anything'. You have to show that you understand what is required of the job you are applying for, what it is about it that appeals to you and what you have to offer. The last bit should be a lot easier as you've had a chance to extend your life experience – but you need to work hard on analysing and describing what you have gained from your time out.

Harry – Thanks for your help but I've come back in July and missed the closing dates for many of the major graduate training schemes.

Jane – Just thought I'd add my bit! I had fixed in my mind that employers only recruited once a year – and was getting rather panic stricken. I was in Nepal, instead of filling in forms in the UK. When I got back, however, I took myself back to my university careers service and got a few facts right. Employers who recruit graduates vary in when they'll accept applications. There are those who stick to a fairly regular cycle – vacancies advertised from November through to February, interviews from Christmas to just after Easter. These tend to be quite a few of the major, national companies so if you are thinking, for example, of personnel or marketing with a large national firm that recruits graduates regularly you are likely to have missed the boat by July. One or two graduate possibilities, such as the Civil Service, have only one or two recruitment dates a year. There will be others, however, that recruit throughout the year so make sure you know who they are.

Ed – Hi to everyone. I just wanted to add that even major companies can not always fill vacancies with applicants of the right calibre and you may be able to pick up some late vacancies, especially in shortage areas, at the graduate summer fairs (your nearest university careers service can tell you when and where they are). That's how I managed to find my current job.

Harry – But what else can I do?

Ed – Friends of mine from university went to work for a range of employers. Don't forget that literally thousands – perhaps the majority – of vacancies in small and medium-sized companies are not recruited this way. If you are thinking of work in tourism, public relations or publishing – or any competitive post in comparatively small companies – you need to be prepared to make speculative applications and to look in relevant trade and professional journals and the local press throughout the year.

Is it worth it?

You should now have been able to decide if time out is for you or not – but at what cost? You've read around some ideas, talked to people and come up with some initial plans and costings. Planning a year off takes quite a lot of work. If, by now, you are still interested in the idea of a gap year . . .

 Next step

Think about your preferred plan for the year, and add more details.

Use the checklists in Chapter 10 – Factfile – to help.

MAKING THE MOST OF IT ALL
9

Think ahead

You've decided to take the plunge! Having persuaded family, teachers and yourself that a year out is a good idea, now is the time to think ahead to when it's over!

In retrospect, that initial shock about the sanitation, the close friend you hated at first sight, the sheer terror of having to teach a class . . . all these will have faded into a haze of later, hopefully more positive, memories.

You will forget how you felt and how you coped. Rachel did:

'I packed so much into my gap year, by the time it got to the end I'd forgotten what happened at the beginning.'

Similarly, it is possible to focus on the boring, repetitive nature of a 'job for money' and overlook what you were learning about time management, working with people from different backgrounds to yourself and coping with difficult members of the public.

'It was only a bar job!'

Does it matter anyway?

Family and friends will be delighted to hear rambling travellers' tales (up to a point!), or hilarious episodes from your work in the supermarket, but future employers will be looking for more insight. They will ask:

'Why did you decide to do it?'
'Did it turn out as you expected/hoped? Why not?'
'How did you cope with difficulties and disappointments?'
'How did you adjust to changing conditions?'
'What did you learn about yourself, especially in relating to others?'

Current application forms of big companies include the following questions. You need to find evidence from your experiences to answer them.

Please describe an occasion when you have successfully persuaded a group or individual of your point of view. How did you achieve this?

Describe a situation where you adopted a new approach to a problem or particular project. What difference did this make?

Please describe the most innovative change you have initiated and what you did to implement this change.

Describe a problem you have had to resolve. How did you achieve this?

Keep a journal

In most areas of education (school, college, university) you are expected to keep a progress file to record and review your learning and experience. This will continue when you get a job, as companies increasingly use appraisal schemes to review your performance and possibly your salary.

Try not to see these as unnecessary chores – use them to advantage! We all find it difficult to put into words what we are good at, how we have developed, our style of solving problems etc. Building up a record, however brief, of all this can be of immeasurable benefit – both to help you make appropriate decisions about the 'next step' and in making a positive impression at future interviews.

If you are convinced about the merits of keeping a journal, follow the steps below:

Three steps to making the most of it all

| Step 1 |
| Before you go |

Start your journal with a list of reminders:

- **Why am I doing this?**
- **How do I hope it will fit into my plans?**
- **What do I hope to achieve?**

| Step 2 |
| During your time out |

Decide on what you want to record – however informally – during your time out, and how often you will review/summarise it.

Useful headings for the review might include:

- **Personal skills** – what am I learning about my personal skills or limitations? What have I learned about how I cope with difficulties? What situations do I find easy or difficult? How well do I relate to people?
- **Language and culture** – if your time out takes you abroad, what impact is this having on you? How far are you enhancing your language skills? How well do you fit into the culture? What do you find difficult? What insights does it give you into your own country, by comparison?
- **Career development** – it's easy to say that time out will help you to firm up your career plans – much harder in practice, when you are travelling around Australia, building a church in South America or working at a supermarket check-out. What have you learned about the kind of organisation you would like to work in? What skills and values do you want your job to enable you to develop?
- **Subject-related** – is this extending my knowledge of my subject?
- **Learning skills** – what am I finding out about my own learning style? How do I best take on board new things? How do I feel now about university or training?

**Step 3
As you return**

When you are coming to the end of your time out, pull it all together.

Make one summary of all the reflections in Step 2. No admissions tutor or employer is likely to want to read it, however brilliantly written or illustrated, but your summary could be a personal 'aide-memoire' that will inform your ability to:

- **make creative career decisions**
- **express yourself well in responding to those difficult questions about yourself on application forms and at interview**

- **ensure that you have gained some familiarity with the recording and reviewing process which, whatever it is called, is now very likely to be part of your education and employment experience in the future.**

 Next step

Focus your career plans, find out how and when the occupation of your choice recruits – and don't despair. There are still plenty of opportunities, providing you learn when and how to present yourself.

Read Chapters 6 and 7 on University/College Views and Employers' Views and use the information resources and websites listed in Chapter 10 – Factfile.

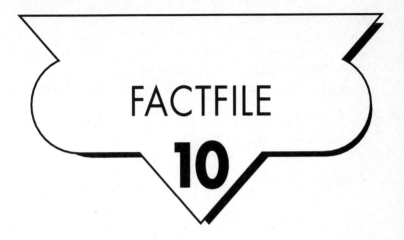

FACTFILE

10

Checklists – things to remember

Once you have decided a year off is for you, use these checklists
to help you get started with your planning. Tick the things that
need checking out. Use the information resources listed in
Infopoint to help.

Going abroad

Basics

☐ Make sure your parents have power of attorney to act on
your behalf re university offers, finance etc.

☐ Getting adequate insurance (health and belongings) is a
MUST! Search around for the best (not necessarily cheapest)
deal.

☐ Decide whether you want a 'round the world' ticket or
whether to 'go as you please' – you may want to change your
itinerary en route. Take advice from the travel specialists, eg
STA Travel.

- [ ] Up-to-date passport.
- [ ] Check visa regulations.
- [ ] Pick up a T6 leaflet (Health Advice) from your post office.
- [ ] Check health regulations, and get the necessary vaccinations.
- [ ] Does your driving licence cover you to drive where you're going?
- [ ] Take a travel guide book with you such as published by Lonely Planet or Rough Guides.

Keeping in touch

Whether you are working abroad, doing voluntary work or travelling, you will need to set up arrangements to keep in touch. This is especially helpful when things go wrong.

- [ ] Set up an e-mail address for yourself and all those you want to keep in touch with.
- [ ] E-mail yourself details of essential contacts – as an extra to keeping paper copies with you and leaving a set with parents.
- [ ] Research phone cards and chargecards.
- [ ] Research the 'post restante' system (available through post offices worldwide).
- [ ] Agree a system of keeping in touch with your family – not too rigid, as you may not have access to a phone/Internet point on the specific day you agreed to make contact.

Work abroad

- [ ] Do you need a work permit?
- [ ] Contact embassies to check any regulations relating to your working in another country.
- [ ] Can you get work organised before you go?
- [ ] What kinds of jobs are you likely to be able to get?
- [ ] Try and arrange accommodation before you go.
- [ ] Would a foreign language help? (Take a crash course.)
- [ ] Have you got any contacts you can use, friends of friends, distant relatives etc?
- [ ] If you get a permanent job and get removal expenses/fares

paid, check what would happen if you want to return home;
you may be asked to pay it back.

☐ Have you got an up-to-date CV? Take it with you or e-mail it
to yourself.

Travel/holidays

☐ Read up as much as you can on the countries you plan to visit
– climate, safety, dress code.

☐ Contact UK branches of embassies and tourist offices and get
as much information as you can.

☐ Decide whether to go alone or seek out a travelling
companion.

☐ Be prepared for your best-laid plans to change as you hear of
interesting places to add to your itinerary.

☐ Accept that other cultures differ, be prepared for both
friendliness and hostility, dress appropriately for the country
you are in, and respect religious customs too.

☐ Take some phrase books if you feel the need and can cope
with the weight!

☐ On the other hand, travel as light as possible; you can pick up
cheap clothing as you go.

☐ Think about security of valuables, take a body purse or some
other means of keeping your passport and money safe.

☐ Use travellers cheques rather than carry large amounts of
cash.

☐ Take a debit/credit card for emergency use.

Voluntary work abroad

☐ Ask your teachers if anyone has had a gap year with the
organisation in the past.

☐ For registered charities, contact the Charity Commission,
which will tell you if the charity has a sound financial basis.

☐ Check if they are a member of the Year Out Group, recently
set up to promote quality experiences for gap years.

☐ Ask for details of ex- and current volunteers you can talk to.

☐ Find out if they have any partnership organisations and speak to them.

☐ Ask about insurance and health requirements.

☐ Are there any age limits?

☐ Do you need to get some qualifications or experience before you are accepted?

☐ Do you have to pay any contribution to get a placement?

☐ Ask where any money you are paying goes.

☐ How long are you prepared to commit yourself to a project?

☐ Do you need to learn at least a few words of the language?

☐ Do you get free board and lodging?

☐ Do you get paid an 'allowance'?

☐ What are living conditions like? Expect the worst!

☐ Do they have repatriation arrangements – so you will be able to get home in an emergency?

☐ Check whether you'd be working on your own or with other volunteers; you may prefer the company.

☐ Do you get any introductory training/acclimatisation on arrival?

Staying in the UK

Voluntary work at home

☐ Check out the wide range of voluntary jobs available through Volunteer Bureaux.

☐ Decide whether you wish to stay local or go elsewhere in the UK.

☐ Choose the placement either for enjoyment or for its work experience value.

☐ Check out the accommodation that's on offer.

☐ Will you be paid an allowance, as well as board and lodging?

☐ Check out the implications if you are claiming any state benefits.

☐ Find out whether you'll be working alone or with others or if you will be supervised.

Employment

☐ Do you know your National Insurance number? You'll need it.

☐ Have you got an up-to-date CV?

☐ Check your tax position with your employer. Make sure you pay it – you'll get some back if you go to college halfway through a tax year.

☐ Check out the pay, hours and other conditions of service, and make sure they suit you.

☐ With some jobs you may be able to take more qualifications while working, or you could take resits or extra examinations at evening class or through e-learning if you need to.

☐ Remember to register with a Jobcentre Plus office if you are unemployed.

☐ If you are out of work for a while, research the local training provision. Jobcentre Plus offices will have details.

Short courses – at home or abroad

☐ Be prepared to pay fees – if so, shop around to find out what different colleges charge.

☐ If you don't take a local course you may need to find accommodation; check it out first.

☐ Try and check on the validating bodies of any course you do; make sure they are bona fide. If in doubt get advice from your careers service or Connexions service.

Infopoint – sources of information and contacts

The sections contain (in this order):

 books

 websites

contact details for the organisations offering opportunities. There are scores of other organisations listed in some of the books referred to under Infopoint.

1. General – careers information
2. General – gap years
3. Travel
4. Work in the UK
5. Work – UK and abroad
6. Work abroad
7. Voluntary work in the UK
8. Voluntary work – UK and abroad
9. Voluntary work abroad
10. Study abroad
11. Study in the UK.

Publishers' addresses are given on page 148–150.

The following organisations provided profiles for *Taking a Year Off*:

BUNAC
Community Service Volunteers
ICYE (Inter-Cultural Youth Exchange)
JET Programme
Karen Hilltribes Trust
Raleigh International
Year in Industry

Contact details are listed in the appropriate section of Chapter 10, Factfile – Infopoint.

1. General – careers information

Jobs and Careers after A levels and Equivalent Advanced Qualifications (Beryl Dixon). Lifetime Careers (Student Helpbook Series)
– information on the dos and don'ts of jobhunting, plus training opportunities.

Occupations. Connexions Service National Unit (formerly COIC)
– comprehensive careers encyclopaedia, with information on a wide range of career choices, including notes on mature entry.

Doctorjob
www.doctorjob.com
– online careers information.

Prospects
www.prospects.ac.uk
– online careers information for graduates.

2. General – gap years

A Year Off ... A Year On? (D'Ath, Doe, Evans and Steel). Lifetime Careers (Student Helpbook Series)
– covers all the options and gives details of organisations offering opportunities.

Before You Go – The Ultimate Guide to Planning Your Gap Year (Tom Griffiths). Aspect Guides
– useful guide to ensure an enjoyable gap year. Includes a Web directory. Tom Griffiths founded the Gap Year Company.

Making the Most of Your Gap Year (Margaret Flynn). Trotman
– a short guide with essential facts to help you decide about gap years.

Opportunities in the Gap Year (Anna Alston). Hobsons/ISCO Publications
– for sixth formers planning a pre-university gap year (see www.gap-year.com).

Planning Your Gap Year (Mark Hempshell). How To Books
– what you can do, where you can go and how to prepare to make the most of the experience.

Spending a Year Abroad. How To Books
– practical advice on what to do, with information on organisations and contact addresses. Includes accounts of people who have taken a year out.

Taking a Gap Year (Susan Griffith). Vacation Work Publications
– details of specialist gap year programmes, jobs, voluntary work, courses and travel opportunities.

Taking a Year Out (Polly Bird). Hodder & Stoughton
– ideas on planning. Lists about 200 work, study, travel, voluntary and expedition options.

Taking a Year Out (Nick Vendome). How To Books
– opportunities for employment, study, volunteer work, independent travel.

The Gap Year Guidebook (Susannah Hecht). John Catt Educational
– further study, job opportunities, advice and contacts, overseas projects including voluntary and paid work.

Gap Year Company
www.gapyear.com
– includes advice, chatrooms, message boards and lots of useful tips for 'gappers'.

Gap-Year
www.gap-year.com
– includes useful advice and directories of organisations involved in gap year activities both in the UK and abroad.

Year Out Group
www.yearoutgroup.org
– detailed advice on gap year and directory of organisations.

3. Travel

Hostelling International Guides. YHA Customer Services
– in two volumes; contains addresses and details of hostels in Europe and the Med (vol. 1), America, Africa, Asia and the Pacific (vol. 2). The website at www.yha.org.uk links to Scotland, Northern Ireland and beyond.

Lonely Planet Guides. Lonely Planet
– guides for most countries in Asia and for many more in Africa, Australasia and North and South America. Website: www.lonelyplanet.com.

Rough Guides
– a series of over 200 practical handbooks covering destinations from Amsterdam to Zimbabwe. Website: www.roughguides.com.

Travellers' Survival Kit – Western Europe. Vacation Work
Publications
– full of practical advice and information for travellers. Details of
the road systems, where to find help and information, border
formalities, when shops and banks open, how to use public
telephones and transport and more.

(Other titles in this series are available for the US and
Canada, Cuba, South America, Central America, Australia and
New Zealand, Russia and the Republics, eastern Europe, Oman
and the Arabian Gulf, the Far East, Lebanon, India, South Africa,
Mauritius, Seychelles and Réunion, Sri Lanka, Mozambique,
Madagascar and Comoros.)

The Virgin Travellers' Handbook (Tom Griffiths). Virgin Books
– whether you're planning a gap year, an extended holiday or
the trip of a lifetime, this guide covers it.

Working Holidays Abroad (Mark Hempshell). Trotman
– travel and pay your way with holiday and part-time work,
plus contact addresses and the type of work available country by
country.

Hostelling
www.hostels.com
– Internet guide to hostelling worldwide with over 1000 hostels.

Know before you go
www.fco.gov.uk (Foreign and Commonwealth Office)
– detailed up-to-date travel advice.

Objective Gap Years
www.objectivegapyear.com
– new organisation offering one-day safety and security
awareness training (price £150) for people going on a gap year.

STA Travel
www.statravel.com
– student travel specialist.

Trailfinders
www.trailfinder.com
– travel specialist.

Travel with Care
www.travelwithcare.co.uk
– general travel advice and travel products for sale.

International Student Identity Card (ISIC)
ISIC Mail Order, Dernier ID, Unit 192, Louis Pearlman Centre,
Goulten Street, Hull HU3 4DL. Tel: 01625 413200. E-mail:
enquiries@nussl.co.uk. Website: www.isiccard.com
– travel and leisure discounts for students.

Leaflet T6
Health Advice for Travellers includes application form for E111
(Health Care in Europe)
– free from post offices or Freephone Healthline 0800 555777.

Rail Europe
Rail Europe House, 34 Tower View, Kings Hill, West Malling,
Kent ME19 4ED. Tel: 08705 848 848. Website:
www.raileurope.co.uk
– specialists in European Rail travel including Inter-rail, France
Railpass, ScanRail and Euro Domino.

Under 26 European Youth Cards
England: National Youth Agency, 17–23 Albion Street, Leicester
LE1 6GD. Tel: 0116 285 3785. E-mail: jonb@nya.org.uk. Website:
www.youthinformation.com.

Wales: Canllaw Online, Caerphilly Business Park, Block A, Van Court, Van Road, Caerphilly CF83 3ED. Tel: 02920 887 868. E-mail: <u>euro26@canllaw-online.com</u>. Website: <u>www.canllaw-online.com</u>.
Northern Ireland: EYC/Usit NOW, Fountain Centre, 13B College Street, Belfast BT1 6ET. Tel: 028 9032 7111. E-mail: <u>youth@usitworld.com</u>. Website: <u>www.youthcard.net</u>.
Scotland: (Young Scot Card and Under 26 European Youth Card), Young Scot, Rosebery House, 9 Haymarket Terrace, Edinburgh EH12 5EZ. Tel: 0131 313 2488. Website: <u>www.youngscot.org</u>.

4. Work in the UK

Summer Jobs in Britain (Jones and Woodworth). Vacation Work Publications
– annually published, lists more than 30,000 vacancies in Britain. Includes sports coaching, farming, childcare, archaeological digs and more plus some vacation traineeships providing work experience. Details of wages, conditions and qualifications needed are given, together with names and addresses of employers.

Careers Advice
<u>www.connexions.gov.uk</u>
– previously local careers services, provides guidance and support to 13–19-year-olds.

Department for Work and Pensions
www.dfwp.gov.uk
– support and advice on work, benefits and pensions.

Fish4jobs
www.fish4jobs.co.uk
– job vacancies in local and regional newspapers.

Jobcentre Plus
www.jobcentreplus.gov.uk
– help and advice on job hunting, benefits and allowances.

Worktrain
www.worktrain.gov.uk
– national jobs and learning.

Year in Industry
Gisbert Kapp Building, University of Birmingham, Edgbaston,
Birmingham B15 2TT. Tel: 0121 414 8116. E-mail:
E_West_Midlands@yini.org.uk. Website: www.yini.org.uk
– industrial placements in local firms: engineering/IT/
business/science related (18–19 years, pre-university only; apply
to local regions – listed on website).

Youth Hostels Association
Trevelyan House, Dimple Road, Matlock, Derbyshire DE4 3YH.
Tel: 01629 592600. E-mail: recruitment@yha.org.uk. Website:
www.yha.org.uk
– domestic/catering/general assistants in hostel accommodation
– around 400 vacancies per year. Website has information on
voluntary activities in countryside and fundraising (eg Cycle
Challenge in Cuba).

5. Work – UK and abroad

Army Gap Year Commission
Tel: 0345 300111. Website: www.army.mod.uk (search on 'gap year')
– benefit from a taste of life in the Regular Army, with no commitment to join (18–20 years, pre-university only).

Interspeak
Stretton Lower Hall, Stretton, Cheshire SK14 7HJ. Tel: 01829 250641. E-mail: post@interspeak.co.uk
– stages (from 1–24 weeks) in companies in the UK, France, Germany and Spain.

PGL Ltd
Alton Court, Penyard Lane, Ross-on-Wye, Herefordshire HR9 5GL. Tel: 01989 767833. E-mail: recruitment@pgl.co.uk. Website: www.pgl.co.uk/personnel
– activity holidays for children in Britain and France. Jobs: instructional, childcare, support, language, catering, admin and senior posts.

Smallpeice Trust
Holly House, 74 Upper Holly Walk, Leamington Spa, Warwickshire CV32 4JL. Tel: 01926 333200. E-mail: info@smallpeicetrust.org.uk. Website: www.smallpeicetrust.org.uk
– offers work experience in the UK and a placement in Europe.

3D Education and Adventure Ltd
Recruitment Department, Osmington Bay Centre, Shortlake Lane, Weymouth, Dorset DT3 6EG. Tel: 01305 836226. E-mail: admin@3d-jobs.co.uk. Website: www.3d-education.co.uk
– instructors on activity/educational holidays for young people in the UK and Europe.

6. Work abroad

The Au Pair and Nanny's Guide to Working Abroad. Vacation Work
Publications
– lists over 280 agencies for nannies, mothers' helps and au pairs.
Details of training and experience required, regulations, health
and insurance in 24 countries. Includes articles on looking after
children, cooking and first aid.

Directory of Jobs and Careers Abroad (Elizabeth Roberts). Vacation
Work Publications
– a guide to permanent career opportunities abroad, for those
who decide they enjoyed their year out so much they want to
stay, and careers information for those in the professions. Covers
Europe, Australia, New Zealand, US, Canada etc.

Directory of Work and Study in Developing Countries (Toby Milner).
Vacation Work Publications
– covers employment, voluntary work and study opportunities
in the developing world. Lists over 400 organisations in over 100
countries. Long- and short-term opportunities in many
countries, including the Caribbean, Latin America, the Middle
East, Africa, the Pacific and the Far East. Looks at engineering,
healthcare, disaster relief, agriculture, teaching, archaeology,
business, economics, oil, irrigation etc.

Eurofacts. Careers Europe
– a series of factsheets about working and studying in European
countries. Includes labour market information for individual
member states, voluntary work opportunities and details of
specific occupations such as au pair work.

Getting a Job Abroad/in Australia/New Zealand/Canada/
Europe. How To Books
– a handbook to help you find short-term or permanent

employment. Includes information on pay, conditions and immigration.

Internships USA. Peterson's Guides, available from Vacation Work
– details of over 50,000 short-term work experience opportunities in the US. Includes business, communications, scientific and other opportunities. Also information on work permit requirements and how to apply.

Living and Working in . . . How To Books
– information on a country-by-country basis. Living and Working in: France, Spain, Portugal, Italy, Germany, The Netherlands, Greece, Scandinavia, Australia, New Zealand, Canada, America and Saudi Arabia.

Live and Work in . . . Vacation Work Publications
– a series of detailed guides on the US/Canada, Scandinavia, Australia/NewZealand, Germany, France, Italy, Spain/Portugal, Belgium/The Netherlands/Luxembourg. Each one tells you what to expect when living in one of these countries, and includes information on accommodation, health, education and employment. Major employers and sources of seasonal work are listed.

Summer Jobs Abroad (Collier and Woodworth). Vacation Work Publications
– lists over 30,000 opportunities with employers around the world. Covers over 50 countries. Jobs for windsurfing instructors, bar staff, bulb-packers, chefs, English teachers, farm-hands, conservationists and so on. Gives details of jobs, period of work required and wages, plus full addresses; also includes information on work permits, visas and health insurance. Includes some winter jobs too.

Summer Jobs USA. Vacation Work Publications
– information on over 55,000 summer jobs in the US; anything from arts and crafts instructors to washers-up. Gives details and wages of board and lodging, also visa and other legal requirements for working in America.

Teaching English Abroad (Susan Griffith). Vacation Work Publications
– guide to short- and longer-term opportunities for both trained and untrained teachers of English as a Foreign Language.

Work Your Way Around the World (Susan Griffith). Vacation Work Publications
– for the traveller who wishes to work en route. Suggestions of how to find work in advance, or when you're out there. Covers grape-picking, teaching, au pairing, catering and so on. Also shows how to 'work a passage', and how to survive when the money runs out. Includes opportunities worldwide.

Working Abroad – The Complete Guide to Overseas Employment (G Golzen and J Reuvid). Kogan Page
– a country-by-country guide covering the economy, working conditions and more in each country.

Working Abroad. AGCAS/CSU information booklet
– contains information on a range of opportunities including voluntary and paid short-term employment throughout the world.

Working in Europe – First Steps. AGCAS/CSU information booklet
– a guide for higher education students and recent graduates who wish to work in Europe that includes information on ways of finding work and an overview of graduate employment trends in 14 countries.

Working Holidays Abroad (Mark Hempshell). Trotman
– see section on Travel.

Working in Ski Resorts – Europe and North America (Victoria
Pybus). Vacation Work Publications
– information about jobs as a ski instructor, chalet worker,
teacher, au pair, resort representative and many more in 80
different resorts. Help with applying via ski tour operators,
school party organisers and others.

Working in Tourism, the UK, Europe and Beyond (Verite Reily
Collins). Vacation Work Publications
– where to find seasonal (and permanent) work in the travel and
tourism industry worldwide.

European Union
www.eures-jobs.com
– database of job vacancies in Europe.

Newspaper links
www.kidon.com/media-link
www.thepaperboy.com
– links to a large number of newspapers and their job vacancies
worldwide.

Overseas Jobs
www.overseasjobs.com
– vacancies around the world.

BUNAC
16 Bowling Green Lane, London EC1R 0QH. Tel: 020 7251 3472.
Website: www.bunac.org.
– opportunities for work in the US and worldwide.

Canvas Holidays
East Port House, Dunfermline, Fife KY12 7JG. Tel: 01383 629000.
Website: www.canvas.co.uk
– campsite supervisors, montage assistants and children's
couriers in western Europe.

Council Exchanges
52 Poland Street, London W1F 7AB. Tel: 020 7478 2000. E-mail:
infouk@councilexchanges.org.uk. Website:
www.councilexchanges.org.uk
– offers work abroad in the US, Australia, Canada and China.

First Choice Overseas Ski Dept
London Road, Crawley, West Sussex RH10 2GX. Tel: 01293
588585. E-mail: skijobs@firstchoice.co.uk. Website:
www.fcski.co.uk.

Holidaybreak Plc
Tel: 01606 787522. Website: www.holidaybreakjobs.com
– camp-site organisers and helpers throughout western Europe
(Eurocamp, Keycamp and Sunsites).

Horizon HPL
Signet House, 49–51 Farringdon Road, London EC1M 3JB. Tel:
020 7404 9192. E-mail: horizonhpl.london@btinternet.com.
Website: http://perso.club-internet.fr/horizon1/
– improve your French on placements in hotels and commercial
companies throughout France.

JET Programme
c/o Council Exchanges, 52 Poland Street, London W1V 4JQ.
Tel: 020 7478 2010. E-mail: jetinfo@councilexchanges.org.uk.
Website: www.councilexchanges.org.uk and
www.jetprogramme.co.uk
– teaching English in Japan (postgraduate only).

Jobs in the Alps
17 High Street, Gretton, Northamptonshire NN17 3DE. Tel: 01536
771150. E-mail: enquiries@jobs-in-the-alps.com. Website:
www.jobs-in-the-alps.com
– work in hotels and restaurants (good French/German required
for most jobs).

Simply Ski
Kings House, Wood Street, Kingston upon Thames KT1 1SG.
Tel: 020 8541 2200. E-mail: ski@simplytravel.com. Website:
www.simply-travel.co.uk.

Ventureco Worldwide Ltd
The Ironyard, 64–66 Market Place, Warwick CV34. Tel: 01926
411122. Fax: 01926 411133. Website:
www.ventureco-worldwide.com.

7. Voluntary work in the UK

Voluntary Agencies Directory. National Council for Voluntary
Organisations (NCVO)
– directory of organisations.

Charity Commission
www.charity-commission.gov.uk
– detailed database of registered charities and their work.

Community Service Volunteers (CSV)

237 Pentonville Road, London N1 9NJ. Tel: 020 7278 6601. E-mail: volunteer@csv.org.uk. Freephone: 0800 374 991. Website: www.csv.org.uk
– social care work of all kinds.

Independent Living Alternatives

Trafalgar House, Grenville Place, London NW7 3SA. Tel: 020 8906 9265. E-mail: mail@I-L-A.fsnet.co.uk. Website: www.I-L-A.fsnet.co.uk
– personal care assistance for disabled people in their own homes.

Oxfam

274 Banbury Road, Oxford OX2 7DZ. Tel: 01865 311311. Website: www.oxfam.org.uk
– office placements in administration, campaigning and retailing (mostly postgraduate).

Prince's Trust Volunteers

18 Park Square East, London NW1 4LH. Tel: 020 7543 1234
– promotes teamwork through outdoor activities and working with disadvantaged young people.

Sue Ryder Foundation

Cavendish, Sudbury, Suffolk CO10 8AY. Tel: 01787 280653/280252/281600
– wide range of opportunities, especially personal care in homes for the sick and disabled.

Treloar Trust

Upper Froyle, Alton, Hampshire GU34 4JX. Tel: 01420 547400. Website: www.treloar.org.uk
– volunteer placements in classrooms, medical centres and sports

and therapy departments. Helping with the care and education of young people with disabilities.

Volunteer Bureaux
Tel: 020 7925 2530. Website: www.do-it.org.uk
– includes addresses of local Volunteer Bureaux nationwide, who can help with finding locally based voluntary work.

8. Voluntary work – UK and abroad

National Centre for Volunteering
www.volunteering.org.uk
– online resource for potential volunteers.

L'Arche
10 Briggate, Silsden, Keighley, West Yorkshire BD20 9JT. Tel: 01535 656186. E-mail: info@larche.org.uk. Website: www.larche.org.uk
– living and working with learning disabled people – mostly in the UK; some opportunities overseas.

Association of Camphill Communities
Gawain House, 56 Welham Road, Norton, North Yorkshire YO17 9DP. Tel: 01653 694197. E-mail: info@camphill.org.uk. Website: www.camphill.org.uk
– living in communities throughout the UK assisting adults with learning disabilities; some placements abroad.

ATD Fourth World
48 Addington Square, London SE5 7LB. Tel: 020 7703 3231.
E-mail: atd@atd-uk.org. Website: www.atd-uk.org
– working with the very poor and disadvantaged in the UK and
western Europe.

The Time for God Scheme
2 Chester House, Pages Lane, London N10 1PR. Tel: 020 8883
1504. Website: www.ourworld.compuserve.com/homepages/
time_for_god
– Christian service in a wide range of community activities in the
UK, Europe and the US.

9. Voluntary work abroad

Finding Voluntary Work Abroad. How To Books
– a practical guide to help you check out the skills and
experience needed for all kinds of voluntary work, plus a wide
variety of opportunities throughout the world.

International Voluntary Work (Whetter and Pybus). Vacation Work
Publications
– lists opportunities with over 750 voluntary organisations for
both short-term and long-term volunteer work, residential and
non-residential. Includes the UK organisations that require both
skilled and unskilled people.

Kibbutz Volunteer (Victoria Pybus). Vacation Work Publications
– all you need to know about working on a kibbutz. Lists over
200 different kibbutzim, describes life and the atmosphere to be
expected. Also includes information on other vacation and short-
term work in Israel, from archaeological digs to fruit-picking.

World Service Enquiry Guide. World Service Enquiry
– directory of organisations involved in relief and development.
Also has a useful website: www.wse.org.uk.

Worldwide Volunteering for Young People. How To Books
– information on nearly 800 organisations and 250,000 annual
placements throughout the UK and in 214 countries
worldwide.

Worldwide Volunteering for Young People
www.worldwidevolunteering.org.uk

Africa and Asia Venture
10 Market Place, Devizes, Wiltshire SN10 1HT. Tel: 01380 729009.
E-mail: av@aventure.co.uk. Website: www.aventure.co.uk
– teaching placements and community projects followed by
organised safari.

African Conservation Experience
Applications Department, PO Box 9706, Solihull, West Midlands
B91 3FF. Tel: 0870 241 5816. E-mail: info@ConservationAfrica.net.
Website: www. ConservationAfrica.net
– conservation work on game reserves in Southern Africa
working with conservationists, biologists and game rangers with
African wildlife.

AFS International Youth Development
Leeming House, Vicar Lane, Leeds LS2 7JF. Tel: 0113 242 6136.
E-mail: info-unitedkingdom@afs.org. Website: www.afs.org
– a wide range of community and environmental projects in
Latin America, Africa and Asia, living in a family.

British Council
10 Spring Gardens, London SW1A 2BN. Tel: 020 7389
4596.Website: www.britishcouncil.org/education/students
– language assistantships (postgraduate or after a minimum two
years of university study).

Caledonia Languages Abroad
The Clockhouse, Bonnington Mill, 72 Newhaven Road,
Edinburgh EH6 5QG. Tel: 0131 621 7721. E-mail:
info@caledonialanguages.co.uk. Website:
www.caledonialanguages.co.uk
– voluntary work placements (after intensive language course) in
tourism industry.

Coral Cay Conservation
Volunteer Recruitment, Coral Cay Conservation (CCC), The
Tower, 13th Floor, 125 High Street, Colliers Wood, London SW19
2JG. Tel: 020 7498 6248. E-mail: info@coralcay.org.uk. Website:
www.coralcay.org
– mostly marine expeditions, surveying coral reefs for
conservation purposes – also work in tropical forests.

European Voluntary Service
Connect Youth-ETG, The British Council, 10 Spring Gardens,
London SW1A 2BN. Tel: 020 7389 4030. E-mail:
yec.enquiries@britishcouncil.org. Website:
www.britishcouncil.org/education/connectyouth/programme/
eyp/evs.htm
– a very wide range of social projects in Europe.

Expeditions Advisory Centre
Royal Geographical Society, 1 Kensington Gore, London SW7
2AR. Tel: 020 7591 3030. E-mail: eac@rgs.org. Website:
www.rgs.org
– gruelling scientific expeditions in hostile environments (16½–20
years). Website has links to other organisations recruiting
expedition members.

EIL Cultural and Educational Travel
287 Worcester Road, Malvern, Worcester WR14 1AB. Tel: 01684
562577. E-mail: info@eiluk.org. Freephone: 0800 018 4015.
Website: www.eiluk.org
– community and conservation work, including the Ecuador
Community Service Programme.

Frontier
50–52 Rivington Street, London EC2A 3QP. Tel: 020 7613 2422.
E-mail: info@frontier.ac.uk. Website: www.frontier.ac.uk
– scientific conservation research expeditions in remote areas of
East Africa and South East Asia.

Gap Activity Projects (GAP)
Gap House, 44 Queen's Road, Reading, Berkshire RG1 4BB. Tel:
0118 959 4914. E-mail: volunteer@gap.org.uk. Website:
www.gap.org.uk
– wide range of placements worldwide, including social work,
conservation and teaching (18–19 years).

Gap Challenge
World Challenge Expeditions, Black Arrow House, 2 Chandos
Road, London NW10 6NF. Tel: 020 8278 7200. E-mail:
welcome@world-challenge.co.uk. Website:
www.world-challenge.co.uk
– expeditions and placements, including conservation and
community work, worldwide.

Global Vision International
Tel: 01582 831300. E-mail: info@gvi.co.uk. Website:
www.gvi.co.uk
– environmental, research and community projects worldwide.

Greenforce
11–15 Betterton Street, Covent Garden, London WC2H 9BP. Tel:
0870 770 2646. E-mail: greenforce@btinternet.com. Website:
www.greenforce.org
– marine and land-based conservation projects.

Indian Volunteers for Community Service
12 Eastleigh Avenue, South Harrow HA2 0UF. Tel: 020 8864 4740.
E-mail: enquiries@ivcs.org.uk. Website: www.ivcs.org.uk
– rural development projects in India.

Inter-Cultural Youth Exchange
Latin American House, Kingsgate Place, London NW6 4TA. Tel:
020 7681 0983. E-mail: info@icye.co.uk. Website: www.icye.co.uk
– placements for one year in Latin America, Africa, Asia and
Europe including: environmental and drug rehabilitation
programmes, working with street children, human rights
projects and HIV programmes.

i to i International Projects
9 Blenheim Terrace, Leeds LS2 9HZ. Tel: 0870 333 2332. E-mail:
info@i-to-i.com. Website: www.i-to-i.com
– teaching English in the Third World (i to i run courses); also
conservation work.

Karen Hilltribes Trust
c/o Mrs Penelope Worsley, Midgley House, Heslington, York
YO10 5DX. Tel: 01904 411891. E-mail:
volunteer@karenhilltribes.org.uk. Website:
www.karenhilltribes.org.uk
– working with the Karen people in north-west Thailand
providing water systems, teaching, administration, engineering,
surveys and construction projects. Placements are for a
minimum of six months.

Kibbutz Program
Tel: 03 5246156/03 5278874. E-mail: kpc@vollentir.co.il. Website:
www.kibbutz.org.il
– introduction to communal way of life on Israeli kibbutzim.

Latin Link
Short Term Experience Projects (STEP), 175 Tower Bridge Road,
London SE1 2AB. Tel: 020 7939 9000. E-mail:

communications.uk@latinlink.org. Websites: www.latinlink.org
and www.stepteams.org
– mostly building projects in Latin America, Spain and Portugal
(Christian commitment necessary).

Project Trust
Hebridean Centre, Ballyhough, Isle of Coll, Argyll PA78 6TE. Tel:
01879 230444. E-mail: info@projecttrust.org.uk. Website:
www.projecttrust.org.uk
– wide range of projects in Third World countries (17–19 years).

Quest Overseas
32 Clapham Mansions, Nightingale Lane, London SW4 9AQ. Tel:
020 8673 3313. E-mail: emailus@questoverseas.com. Website:
www.questoverseas.com
– community development and conservation projects and
expeditions in South America and Africa.

Raleigh International
27 Parsons Green Lane, London SW6 4HZ. Tel: 020 7371 8585.
E-mail: info@raleigh.org.uk. Website: www.raleigh.org.uk
– environmental and community projects in remote parts, to
build leadership and teamwork skills.

Right Hand Trust
24 School Street, Wolverhampton WV1 4LF. Tel: 01902 428824.
E-mail: mail@righthandtrust.org.uk. Website:
www.righthandtrust.org.uk
– Christian projects in Africa.

Students Partnership Worldwide
17 Dean's Yard, London SW1P 3PB. Tel: 020 7222 0138. E-mail:
spwuk@gn.apc.org. Website: www.spw.org
– environmental and health projects, working with young people
in developing countries.

Teaching Abroad
Gerrard House, Rustington, West Sussex BN16 1AW. Tel: 01903
859911. E-mail: info@teaching-abroad.co.uk. Website:
www.teaching-abroad.co.uk
– teaching English in many countries. NB: spin-off organisations
Projects Abroad and Business Abroad offer a range of other
opportunities.

Travellers Worldwide
7 Mulberry Close, Ferring, West Sussex BN12 5HY. Tel: 01903
700478. E-mail: info@travellersworldwide.com. Website:
www.travellersworldwide.com
– teaching, conservation and various work experience
placements in many countries.

Trekforce Expeditions (part of International Scientific Support
Trust)
34 Buckingham Palace Road, London SW1W 0RE. Tel: 020 7828
2275. E-mail: info@trekforce@org.uk. Website:
www.trekforce.org.uk
– conservation projects in Belize and Borneo; community projects
in Central America and SE Asia.

10. Study abroad

Directory of Work and Study in Developing Countries
– for details see 'Work abroad'.

Eurofacts. Careers Europe
– see 'Work abroad'.

Experience Erasmus: The UK Guide to Socrates Erasmus programmes.
ISCO Publications
– a comprehensive, annually updated source of information on
programmes associated with the European programme.

International Awards 2001. Association of Commonwealth
Universities
– new directory listing awards tenable at universities in
Commonwealth countries.

The Student Handbook. Kogan Page
– a directory of courses and institutions in higher education for
29 countries that are not members of the European Union.

Study Abroad. UNESCO
– details international courses, fees and scholarships. Edition for
2003/4 due out end of 2002.

AFS International Youth Development
Leeming House, Vicar Lane, Leeds LS2 7JF. Tel: 0113 242 6136.
E-mail: info-unitedkingdom@afs.org. Website: www.afs.org
– live in a family and study for a year abroad (15–18 years at
time of application).

CESA Languages Abroad
Western House, Malpas, Truro, Cornwall TR1 1SQ. Tel: 01872
225300. E-mail: info@cesalanguages.com. Website:
www.cesalanguages.com
– a very wide range of languages in many countries.

Challenge Educational Services
101 Lorna Road, Hove, East Sussex BN3 3EL. Tel: 01273 220261.
E-mail: enquiries@challengeuk.com. Website:
www.challengeuk.com

– French-language programmes in France; academic year in the US (15–18 years) and US work placements.

Council Exchanges
52 Poland Street, London W1F 7AB. Tel: 020 7478 2020. E-mail: infouk@councilexchanges.org.uk. Website: www.councilexchanges.org.uk
– study abroad programmes in Europe, Cuba and Ecuador.

EF International Language Schools
74 Roupell Street, London SE1 8SS. Tel: 08707 200708. E-mail: languages.gb@ef.com. Website: www.ef.com
– foreign language courses in many countries.

English Speaking Union
Dartmouth House, 37 Charles Street, London W1J 5ED. Tel: 020 7529 1550. E-mail: esu@esu.org. Website: www.esu.org.uk
– runs scheme enabling students to live and study in US independent schools (pre-university only).

Euro Academy
24 Clarendon Rise, London SE13 5EY. Tel: 020 8297 0505. E-mail: enquiries@euroacademy.co.uk. Website: www.euroacademy.co.uk
– language courses in many European countries.

Nonstopski
1a Bickersteth, London SW17 9SE. Tel: 020 8772 7852. E-mail: info@nonstopski.com. Website: www.nonstopski.com
– study in Canada for skiing or snowboard instructor qualifications.

11. Study in the UK

CRAC Directory of Further Education (DOFE). Hobsons
– a comprehensive directory of all vocational and academic
further education courses.

ECCTIS
www.ecctis.co.uk
– UK courses directory. Full details only available from
registered sites.

Learndirect
www.learndirect.co.uk
– details online learning opportunities.

Publishers' addresses

Following are contact addresses of publishers of books in the
above lists. Books may normally be obtained through high street
or online bookshops, but may also be available in your school or
college careers library for reference. Similarly, most of the books
mentioned are available in public libraries.

Aspect Guides, 32–34 Great Peter Street, London SW1P 2DB. Tel:
020 7222 1155. E-mail: info@aspectguides.com. Website:
www.aspectguides.com.

Association of Commonwealth Universities, 36 Gordon Square, London WC1H 0PF. Website: www.acu.ac.uk.

AGCAS/CSU Publications Ltd, Despatch Department, Prospects House, Booth Street East, Manchester M13 9EP. Website: www.prospects.ac.uk.

Careers Europe, 3rd Floor, Midland House, 14 Cheapside, Bradford BD1 4JA. Website: www.careerseurope.co.uk.

Connexions Service National Unit (formerley COIC – Careers and Occupational Information Centre). E-mail: connexions@prolog.uk.com. Website: www.connexions.gov.uk.

CRAC Hobsons Publishing PLC, 159–173 St John Street, London EC1V 4DR. Website: www.hobsons.com.

Hodder & Stoughton, Hodder Headline, 338 Euston Road, London NW1 3BH. Website: www.madaboutbooks.com.

How To Books Ltd, 3 Newtec Place, Magdalen Road, Oxford OX4 1RE. Website: www.howtobooks.co.uk.

ISCO Publications, 12a Princess Way, Camberley, Surrey GU15 3SP. Tel 01276 21188. Website: www.isco.org.uk.

John Catt Educational Limited, Great Glemham, Saxmundham, Suffolk IP17 2DH. Tel: 01728 663666. E-mail: info@gap-year.com. Website: www.johncatt.com.

Kogan Page, 120 Pentonville Road, London N1 9JN. Website: www.kogan-page.co.uk.

Lifetime Careers Publishing. E-mail: sales@lifetime-publishing.co.uk. Website: www.lifetime-publishing.co.uk.

Lonely Planet, The Barley Mow Centre, 10a Spring Place, London NW5 3BH. Website: www.lonelyplanet.com.

NCVO Publications, Regent's Wharf, 8 All Saints Street, London N1 9RL. Tel: 020 7713 6161. Website: www.ncvo-vol.org.uk.

Rough Guides, 62–70 Shorts Gardens, London WC2H 9AH. Website: www.roughguides.com.

Trotman and Co Ltd, 2 The Green, Richmond, Surrey TW9 1PL. Website: www.trotmanpublishing.co.uk.

UNESCO. Website: www.unesco.org.

Vacation Work, 9 Park End Street, Oxford OX1 1HJ. Tel 01865 241978. Website: www.vacationwork.co.uk.

Virgin Books. Website: www.Virgin-Books.com.

World Service Enquiry, 233 Bon Marché Centre, 241–251 Ferndale Road, London SW9 8BJ. Tel: 0870 770 3274. E-mail: wse@cabroad.org.uk.

YHA Customer Services, 8 St Stephen's Hill, St Albans, Hertfordshire AL1 2DY. Website: www.yha.org.uk.

ADVERTISERS' INDEX